# MICE
# All about them

by Dr. Alvin Silverstein
and Virginia B. Silverstein

with photographs by Robert A. Silverstein

J.B. Lippincott    New York

All photos courtesy of Robert Silverstein except for the following: p. 8, The Department of Health, City of New York; pp. 12, 33, Wide World Photos; pp. 14, 67, U.S. Fish & Wildlife Service; p. 37, U.S. Bureau of Biological Survey; pp. 40, 125, 133, National Institutes of Health; pp. 48, 53, 56, 58, San Diego Zoological Society; pp. 59, 65, 68–69, Ernest P. Walker; p. 62, Heather Angel; p. 63, Division of Photography, Field Museum of Natural History; p. 66, Karl H. Maslowski; p. 70, V. Bailey, Fish and Wildlife Service; p. 72, Australian News and Information Bureau; p. 75, G. Ronald Austing, National Audubon Society; pp. 90–91, 139, 141, The Jackson Laboratory, Bar Harbor, Maine; p. 131, Thomas D. Luckey.

MICE: All about them
Copyright © 1980 by Alvin and Virginia B. Silverstein
All rights reserved. Printed in the United States of America.
No part of this book may be used or reproduced in any manner
whatsoever without written permission except in the case of
brief quotations embodied in critical articles and reviews.
For information address J. B. Lippincott Junior Books, 10 East 53rd Street,
New York, N.Y. 10022. Published simultaneously in Canada by
Fitzhenry & Whiteside Limited, Toronto.

Designed by Kohar Alexanian

3 4 5 6 7 8 9 10

Library of Congress Cataloging in Publication Data
Silverstein, Alvin.
  Mice, all about them.

  Includes index.
  SUMMARY: Examines the habits, characteristics,
and history of mice. Also includes a discussion of
pet mice and the use of these creatures in folklore,
legend, and literature.
    1. Mice—Juvenile literature. [1. Mice]
I. Silverstein, Virginia B., joint author.
II. Silverstein, Robert A.   III.  Title.
QL737.R6S584     1980      599.32'33      79-9621
ISBN 0-397-31922-3
ISBN 0-397-31923-1 (lib. bdg.)

For Martina and Jenny Barbera

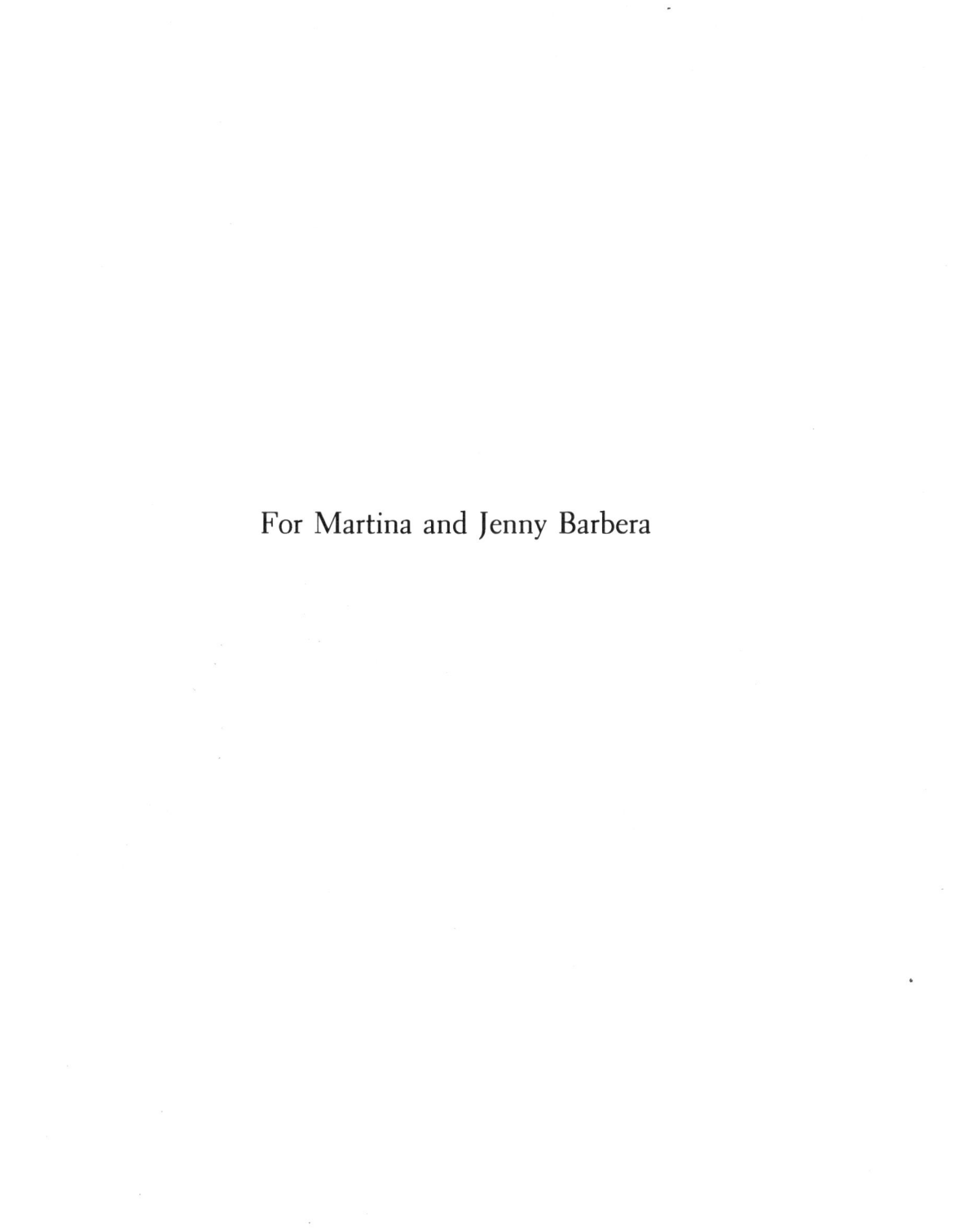

# CONTENTS

| | |
|---|---|
| UNINVITED GUESTS | 1 |
| CREATURES OF LEGEND AND LORE | 20 |
| CHAMPIONS AT SURVIVAL | 34 |
| IN FOREST, FIELD, AND DESERT | 51 |
| THE BALANCE OF NATURE | 73 |
| MICE AS PETS | 85 |
| MICE IN THE LABORATORY | 124 |
| HOW THE RODENTS ARE RELATED | 144 |
| FOR FURTHER READING | 146 |
| INDEX | 147 |

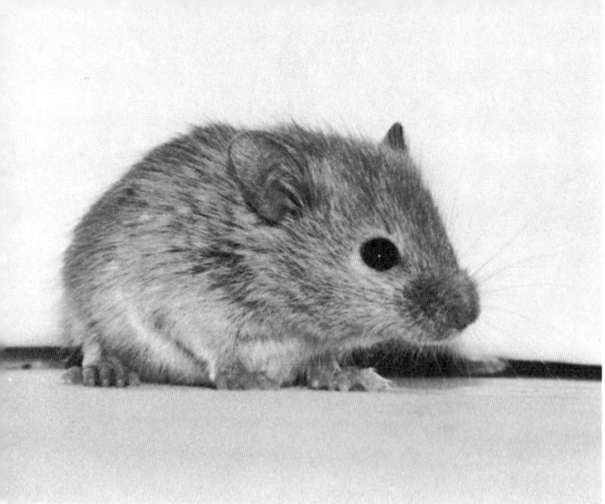
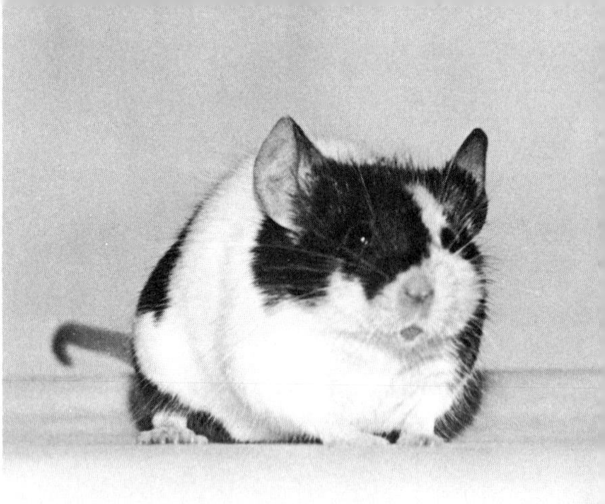
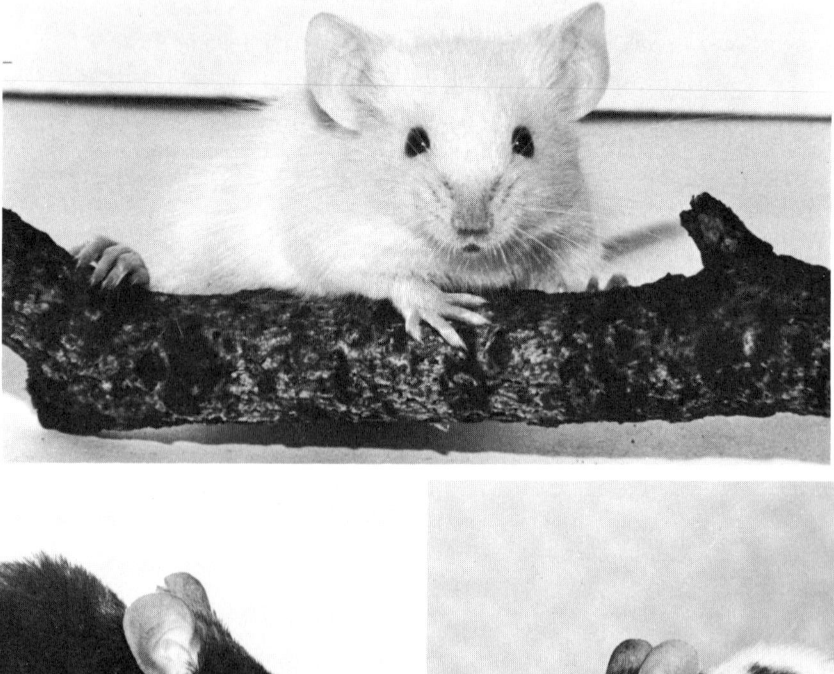
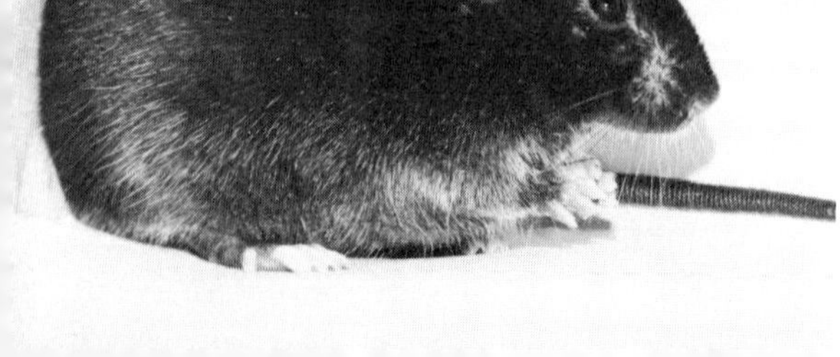
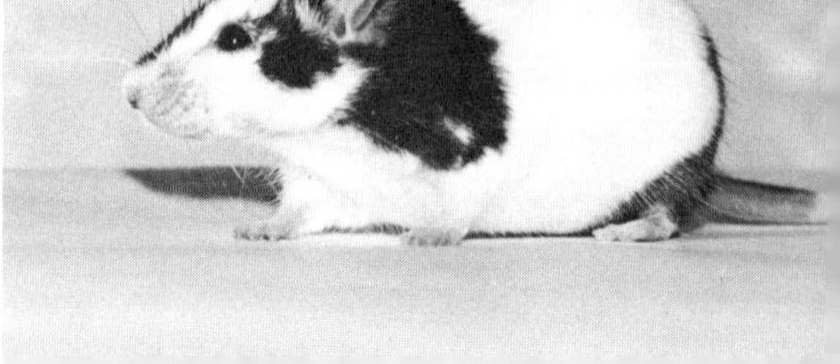

# UNINVITED GUESTS

Some years ago, when we lived in an apartment, we had a habit of working late. Soon we realized that we weren't alone. We'd look up from our books and papers, and there, over by the wall, would sit a little gray mouse, up on its haunches, peering out at us with its bright beady eyes and sniffing with its bewhiskered nose. A sudden move, and it would go scooting away through the gap under the door. But if we worked quietly or even talked softly, it would sit there quite unafraid and sometimes venture farther out into the room.

Night after night our little mouse came to greet us. We were enchanted, and began laying down bits of cheese for it. But then we began to wonder. Some nights the mouse seemed to be bigger than others, and some nights it looked smaller. Then we discovered the corners gnawed off a whole ream of typing paper. By the time we saw *two* mice scampering across the floor, we had already guessed: we didn't have "a mouse"; we had *mice*. And we had a problem!

Our problem was not a very new or unusual one. People have been finding mice in their houses as long as there have been people with houses. In fact, our association with these furry creatures goes back even further. Scientists have found the bones of mice and rats in the same caves in which our ancestors, the cave people, lived.

Nobody knows when mice first moved in to live with humans. The first mice made their homes in fields and forests, and many relatives of today's house mouse still do. But many thousands of years ago, long before the beginnings of recorded history, some of these tiny creatures happened upon an easier life. They discovered that where people lived, there was warmth and shelter from the wind and rain. There was food aplenty. Just the scraps of food that people dropped or threw away could keep a mouse contented, and the extra food that people stored for later use could feed an army of mice.

The early people roamed about, following the herds of animals they hunted and gathering fruits, seeds, and nuts as they ripened. Sometimes mice and rats traveled with them, hidden in packs of clothes or food, or hitching rides in boats. In fact, some of the rats and mice living in Australia today are believed to be descendants of stowaways who sailed across the seas from Asia with the aborigine settlers about ten thousand years ago.

It was about that time that people in various parts of

the world learned to grow crops and store grain. With agriculture, people no longer had to move about continually, but could settle down in one place—a way of life that was convenient for both people and mice. The earliest farming villages that archaeologists have found were located in Asia, in the region that is now northern Iran and Soviet Turkestan. Wild ancestors of the house mouse were common in that region, as well as in the lands around the Mediterranean and across the steppes of Asia to the Far East. As farming practices spread, mice were quick to move into the new settlements. Then, as people migrated, mice traveled with them, spreading all over Europe, Africa, and Asia.

We know that the granaries of ancient Egypt were plagued by mice. The Egyptians believed that mice were born from the mud of the flooding Nile River. Trying to get rid of their uninvited guests, these ancient people welcomed small African wildcats into their homes and storehouses, and eventually domesticated them. Egyptian records dating back to 4500 B.C. show pictures of cats, which were kept on farms, in houses, and in public buildings to catch mice.

Other peoples tried to devise mechanical mousetraps. In Iran, archaeologists have found some small pottery vessels, each with a sliding door at one end held up by a string attached to a bit of bait inside the pot. If a mouse entered the trap and nibbled at the bait, it loosened the string and the door plopped down, shutting the mouse up inside. That design sounds rather like a modern live trap, but the pottery dates back to about 2500 B.C.

Mice are mentioned in many writings from ancient Greece and Rome, and bones of these tiny animals have been found in ruins of buildings of the time. In the first century B.C., the Greek geographer Strabo noticed that epidemics of certain diseases seemed to occur where mice were plentiful, and he suggested that these animals might carry disease. His guess was a shrewd one, but few Greeks of the time shared his opinion of mice. For them the house mouse was a symbol of tenderness, and people called their sweethearts "little mouse."

In some parts of the ancient world, mice were actually worshipped as sacred animals. Other people, however, shared the Egyptians' view and regarded mice as pests. The ancient Hebrews considered mice unclean, and thought they were a punishment from God. The Zoroastrians in Persia taught that killing mice was a service to humanity. The conquering Romans helped to spread cats through Europe, and these animals were prized for their usefulness in protecting homes and storehouses against pests. Old Welsh law set the worth of a cat at a penny from birth until its eyes opened, at two pennies for a kitten not yet old enough to kill mice, and at four pence for a trained mouser. (That may not sound like much today, but in those times a lamb, a kid, a goose, or a hen could be bought for a penny.) In the Far East, too, cats were kept to kill the mice that threatened the grain harvests and the silk industry.

House mice were originally creatures of the Old World. But as people began crossing the oceans and exploring and settling in the Americas, stowaway mice tagged along. Hiding in grain sacks and packages of clothes and tools, scampering nimbly on and off ships along ropes and riggings, they soon

*House mice spread through the world as stowaways.*

established their own colonies in the New World. When covered wagons moved west, mice went along with them. Today these hardy little animals continue to ride ships and trains, trucks and even airplanes, going wherever people go. During World War II, the German general Rommel discovered a nest of mice in his tank in the middle of the North African desert. Explorers in the frozen wastes of the Antarctic have found mice thriving in their packs of supplies.

Wherever house mice have gone, they have met and had to compete with other mouselike creatures. All belong to an enormous group of animals called rodents.

# RODENTS

Like humans, rodents belong to the class of mammals—warm-blooded animals that suckle their young with milk made in their own bodies. Amazingly, there are nearly as many different species of rodents as there are of all other kinds of mammals together. The smallest rodents are mice, which are small enough to sit comfortably in the palm of your hand. The largest rodent in the world is the capybara, a wild relative of the guinea pig that lives in South America. Capybaras look like shaggy pigs; they may grow to be four feet long and may weigh as much as a grown man.

Rodents of various kinds are found everywhere on earth. Burrows in grasslands and meadows are the homes of prairie dogs and gophers. In the forests, squirrels scamper about on the branches of trees, and wood mice nest in hollow trees and logs. Beavers and muskrats are at home in the water, swimming with ease and building lodges of branches and mud in rivers and lakes. In the deserts, many small rodents, such as kangaroo rats and gerbils, can live without ever drinking water.

The name of the rodents comes from a Latin word, *rodere*, that means "to gnaw." This order of mammals is well named. All rodents, from the tiniest mouse to the giant capybara, from the gerbils of the desert to the river-dwelling beavers, have one thing in common. They have sharp teeth, good for gnawing, and a constant need to gnaw on things.

Rodents' teeth are very unusual. Our teeth and those of most other mammals, such as dogs, cats, horses, and cows, grow to a certain size and then stop. The front teeth of rodents never stop growing as long as the animals live; in a tiny mouse the teeth can grow as much as five centimeters (about two inches) in a year. Of course, you don't find mice with two-inch teeth walking around, for their teeth are built not only to grow but also to wear down continually. The front surface is made of enamel, the hardest substance in the body. The back part of each tooth is made of a softer, bonelike substance called dentin. As the rodent bites on things, the dentin wears away, keeping the cutting surfaces of the teeth as sharp as tiny chisels.

*Rodent's teeth are specialized for gnawing. They also make an impressive display, as this angry brown rat shows.*

A rodent's four front teeth (two in the top jaw and two in the bottom) are incisors, or cutting teeth. A mouse may use its incisors to crack open the tough outer coating of seeds and nuts, to bite down on an insect it has caught, or to shred grasses and fibers for bedding to line its nest. The huge incisors of a beaver are strong and sharp enough to chop down trees.

We humans have a total of eight incisors, and in back of them are the pointed canines and a variety of broader teeth. Scientists believe that the ancestors of the rodents had sets of teeth something like ours, but that somewhere along the line some of the teeth were lost. Today's rodents have a wide gap, called a diastema, on each side of their incisors, and then, at the back of the jaws, a set of grinding teeth to chew up the material torn apart by their incisors. A mouse has a total of sixteen teeth—four incisors and twelve molars (grinding teeth).

The order of rodents is divided into three large suborders. The suborder Sciuromorpha, or "squirrel-shaped ones," includes squirrels, prairie dogs, gophers, chipmunks, woodchucks, and beavers. The suborder Hystricomorpha, or "porcupine-shaped" rodents, includes porcupines, guinea pigs and their relatives, and chinchillas. The largest group of rodents is the suborder Myomorpha, "the mouse-shaped ones." Scientists group the mouselike rodents into ten families, including the cricetids ("the squeaking ones"—all the mice and rats native to the New World, plus hamsters, gerbils, lemmings, and muskrats), and the murids ("the mousy ones"—house mice, house rats, and various Old World mice of the woods and fields).

## RATS AND MICE

A variety of fairly small, furry rodents with pointed noses are called rats and mice. These little animals usually have long tails, which may be bare and scaly and longer than their bodies.

Sometimes it is hard to determine whether a particular animal should be called a rat or a mouse. Usually the choice is made on the basis of size: very small rodents are mice, and somewhat larger ones are rats. The common house rat is several times longer than the house mouse, and may weigh more than ten times as much.

Rats and mice come in many different sizes, shapes, and colors, with very different habits and ways of life. The ones we know best are those that make their homes in our houses, stores, warehouses, and sewers, on wharves, and even in ships and trains.

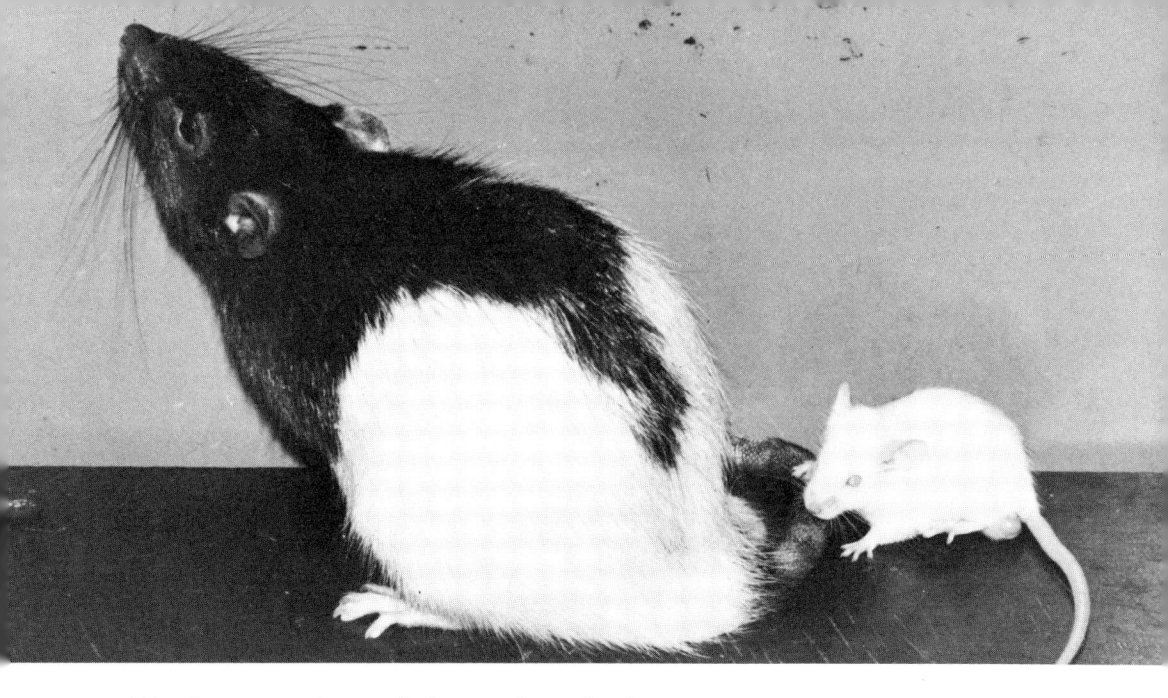

*The house rat is much larger than the house mouse.*

These small rodents build their nests in dark corners, inside walls, or under floorboards. They come out to forage for food, usually at night, and are always on the alert. The slightest sight, sound, or smell of danger sends them scurrying for cover. They eat anything they can find, and their sharp teeth are always ready to sample a likely-looking morsel, even a book or a piece of furniture.

Animals that have adapted to living with another species, sharing food and shelter, are called commensals. This word comes from Latin roots meaning "eating at the same table with." Some of our native mice, such as the white-footed mouse, may occasionally move into people's houses and share their food. But our common rodent commensals are three species of Old World murids that reached the Americas as stowaways on the ships of explorers and settlers: the black and brown rats, and the house mouse.

The first house rats to spread across the world were the black rats, so called because of their glossy black coats. (Another name, roof rats, comes from their habit of living high up in the upper floors of houses.) It is thought that their ancestors were wild rats from the deserts of southern Asia. Gradually they discovered that food and shelter were plentiful in villages and towns, and they began to live with humans in ever-growing numbers. Then came the Crusades of the Middle Ages. Black rats stowed away aboard the ships of

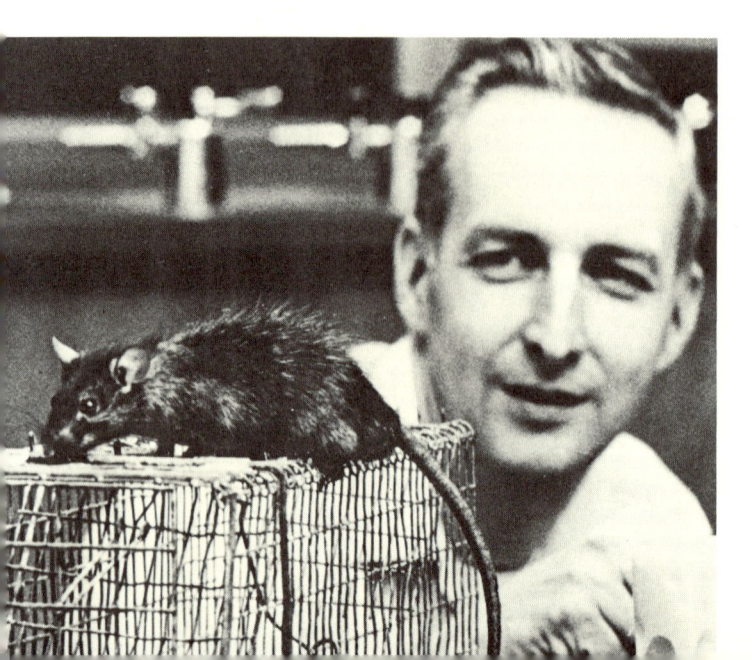

*This black rat is being studied by biologist William B. Jackson.*

Crusaders returning from the Holy Land, and soon had thriving outposts in Europe. From there they sailed in the ships of explorers and settlers to the New World.

With them these small invaders brought disease and death. Fleas, ticks, and lice living on the bodies of the rats sometimes hopped over to humans, carrying disease germs that they injected with their bites. Fleas living on rats carried the dread bubonic plague, which killed millions of people in Europe during the Middle Ages. In one of the worst outbreaks of the so-called Black Death, more than a quarter of the human population died. The people of the time did not realize that rats were an important link in the spread of the plague, but they did know that rats were destructive pests, and they tried to find ways to kill them.

Strangely, the most effective killers of the black rats turned out to be their relatives, the brown rats. These are larger than black rats, with shorter ears and tails and thicker, blunter muzzles. They are thought to have come from somewhere in central Asia. They had never been seen in Europe before the eighteenth century. Then, suddenly and mysteriously, hordes of brown rats began to sweep across the continent. In 1727, armies of brown rats were seen crossing Russia. On the invaders went, hungrily mowing down grain fields and swimming across rivers in their path.

A number of similar mass migrations have been reported in the last few hundred years, and not just among rats. Sometimes a local population of mice, rats, gerbils, or lemmings suddenly starts to multiply so rapidly that rodents fill up all the available space and eat up the entire food supply. Then they move outward, in masses so dense that they carpet the ground with furry bodies. On they go, single-mindedly. The broadest rivers do not stop them; they plunge down the banks and either swim across or drown.

By 1728, a few brown rats had reached England. At the time it was believed that they had stowed away aboard a Norwegian timber ship. Thus, the brown rat received another common name, the Norway rat.

Brown rats soon had thriving colonies in Europe, and from there they spread to America. They arrived around the time of the Revolutionary War and found that the new

*A female brown rat guards her litter in a nest in the corner of a storeroom.*

land had food and shelter in abundance. As the frontiers were opened, brown rats moved west, too, stowing away on covered wagons and in trains.

The brown rat is much fiercer than its black cousin, and wherever the second wave of invaders has passed, black rats have been killed off. Only in the tropics, where the black rat is better fitted to live than the brown rat, are black rats still thriving.

House mice belong to the same family as the black rat and brown rat, but they are much smaller and more timid than their rat cousins. They are delicate, graceful little creatures, with slim bodies and tiny feet. Their forefeet, each with four "fingers" and a little thumb knob, can be used for grasping things as well as for walking. A house mouse's thin, scaly tail is longer than its body. The house mouse may swing or jerk its tail from side to side as it runs, climbs,

*A scaly tail . . .*
*that helps the mouse*
*to balance.*

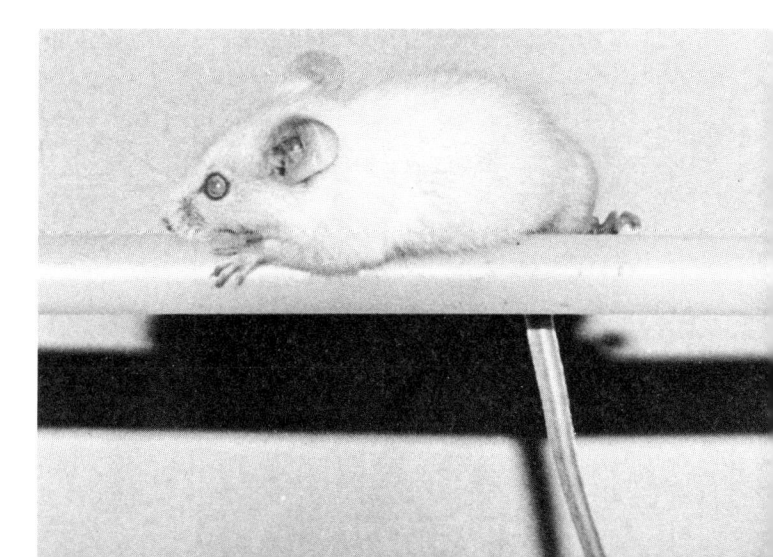

or leaps, helping to keep its balance. (House mice can climb up a brick wall with ease, leap fearlessly across openings, and can jump down from a shelf or up onto a table. They are also good swimmers, though they dislike getting wet and stay out of the water if they have a choice.)

A mouse's scaly tail is also useful in another way. It is a portable thermostat, helping to keep the rodent's body temperature even. When it is very hot outside, a mouse's tail gives off heat, helping to cool its body. When it is cold, the blood vessels in the mouse's tail contract, cutting down the amount of heat that is carried through the tail and lost to the outside.

The bright, beady eyes of a mouse are one of its most striking features. Actually, however, those alert-looking eyes are rather nearsighted. Like most animals that are active mainly at night, mice depend more on other senses to bring them information about the world. They have a keen sense of smell, and sniff continually as they explore new surroundings. People have discovered that mice have a great dislike for certain odors: a sprinkling of naphthalene flakes, for example, will keep stored clothing or books safe from a mouse's nibbling. Other strong-smelling substances, such as sulfur, lime, and cedar, and oils of citronella, peppermint, and wintergreen, also seem to repel mice.

*Bright beady eyes,
a keen nose,
large ears,
and whisker "feelers."*

The whiskers that spread out from a mouse's muzzle are sensitive organs of touch; with them a mouse can feel objects even in the dark, and estimate whether an opening is big enough for its body to pass through. The mouse's large ears are sound funnels, and it has a keen sense of hearing. Any alarming noise will send it instantly scurrying to cover. A mouse can hear sounds far more high-pitched than the highest sounds human ears can hear. Mice also make sounds in this very high-pitched range—the shrill squeaks that we can hear are actually the lowest sounds a mouse makes. (Unfortunately for mice, another night prowler, the cat, also has ears that can hear high-pitched squeakings. Cats can often find mice by tracing the sounds they make.)

The fur of a house mouse is usually a dull gray or brownish

color, slightly lighter on its underparts. Its inconspicuous coloring makes the mouse difficult to spot, and helps to protect it as it scurries about. Occasionally mutations (hereditary changes) occur, and a mouse with different-colored fur is born—perhaps one with fur that is yellow, or black, or spotted, or pure white. For a mouse living wild in forest or fields, unusual-colored fur can be a real disadvantage, decreasing the animal's chance for survival. White fur would be especially easy for a mouse's enemies—owls, for example—to notice against a dark background. And mice living as commensals are easier for people to spot if they have unusual-colored fur. But if a mouse's unusual feature happens to take the fancy of a human, it may help the animal to survive and pass on the new trait. People have been raising unusual mice as pets for thousands of years, breeding them carefully so that their special traits are passed on from generation to generation. When scientists began to use mice as laboratory animals, they went to breeders of "fancy mice" for their laboratory breeding stocks, rather than catching wild mice. These special mouse strains were more predictable and consistent in their reactions to many tests and experiments, since their heredity had been so carefully controlled; and the mice were much gentler, easier to raise, and better adapted to laboratory life than their wild relatives.

The official scientific name for the house mouse is *Mus musculus*—the Latin words translate whimsically as "Mouse Littlemouse." Both the Latin *mus* and our own "mouse" come from an ancient Sanskrit word, *musha*, which means "thief." It is not hard to imagine how the house mouse got that name, for it lives by stealing whatever food it can find in people's houses. House mice can be annoying pests, and sometimes dangerous—like their rat cousins, mice can carry and spread disease. But mice have probably saved more human lives than they have cost. In laboratories throughout the world, mice are being used to study diseases such as cancer and diabetes, to develop and test new drugs, and to learn more about why we and other animals act as we do. These rodents also make lively and gentle pets.

In the thousands of years that humans have been living with mice as uninvited guests, we have learned a great deal about them. Mice, with their typical habits and ways, have crept into our legends and lore, and even into our common speech.

# CREATURES OF LEGEND AND LORE

Expressions such as "quiet as a mouse," "meek as a mouse," and "when the cat's away, the mice will play" have been part of our common speech for a long time. Such expressions usually describe the habits of mice, as people see them. The phrase "poor as a church mouse," for example, is thought to refer to the fact that there is no kitchen or pantry in a church, where a foraging mouse could find convenient scraps of food to eat. A "church mouse" would thus lead a very poor and hungry life, indeed. The common taunt, "Are you a man or a mouse?" is typical of the way mice are pictured in our speech, almost always as timid and shy.

Mice have played important roles in the folklore and legends of many lands, in almost every part of the world, and they have continued to play starring roles in popular literature today. Two major threads seem to run through mouse stories and legends. In some cases, mice are described in the roles they play in our world: sneaking about, stealing bits of food, and spreading filth and disease. In other stories and legends, mice are not really pictured as rodents, but, instead, symbolize human traits that are similar to their own. Very often they symbolize the small and weak of the world.

## AND THE MORAL IS . . .

Aesop, the Greek fable teller who lived from about 620 to 560 B.C., used stories about animals to point up morals that could be applied to human affairs. Some of his most famous tales involve mice. For example, there is the story of the council of mice that met to discuss what to do about a cat that was making their lives miserable and killing many of them. One mouse suggested a simple solution. "All we have to do is tie a bell on the cat. Then, wherever she goes, the tinkling of the bell will give us a warning." All the mice cheered and applauded this brilliant idea. Then one old mouse said quietly, "It is a fine idea, indeed, but who is going to bell the cat?" The wise old mouse in the story points up the moral that it is often far easier to suggest a solution to a problem than to put it into practice.

Another familiar Aesop's fable is the story of the town mouse and the country mouse. Visiting in the country, the town mouse was scornful of the bare living his country friend scratched out (for the country mouse ate only wheat stalks and roots from the hedgerow). The town mouse persuaded the country mouse to come home with him for a real feast. When they arrived, the town mouse laid out such a spread of bread, barley, beans, figs, honey, raisins, and cheese that the country mouse bewailed his own hard life. But each time the two mice began to eat their feast, someone came into the room and the frightened rodents had to run, squeaking, to hide in a hole. At last the country mouse, still hungry, went back to his field. There the food might be plain, but at least he could live without fear.

Another fable tells of a lion and a mouse. The lion awoke one day to find a mouse running over him. With a giant paw he seized the tiny mouse, and was about to eat him. "Let me go," the mouse squeaked, trembling with fear, "and I will repay you someday." The lion was so amused at the idea that a mouse could ever do anything for him that he let the little rodent go.

The lion soon forgot about the mouse—until the day he was caught by hunters and tied firmly with strong ropes. A little mouse came by—the same mouse whose life the lion had spared. The mouse repaid his debt by gnawing through the ropes to free the lion. This famous fable shows that at times even the strongest may need help from the weak.

The mouse is so well suited for making this particular point that similar devices have been used in modern tales. In *The Wizard of Oz,* for instance, Dorothy and her friends were crossing a field of scarlet poppies when the smell of the flowers put them into a deep, deep sleep. Only the Scarecrow and Tin Woodman were unaffected. They carried Dorothy and her little dog Toto to safety but could not budge the heavy Cowardly Lion. They finally hauled him to safety with the help of thousands of tiny field mice, who came to repay the Woodman's kindness to their queen.

This episode shows that the small and weak of the world, by working together, can sometimes accomplish deeds that the strong could not accomplish alone.

MICE EVERYWHERE

Mice have long been accepted as a commonplace part of our world. It is not surprising that many of the tales and rhymes that have been passed down through the generations contain references to them.

In the Mother Goose rhymes, for example, mice are often mentioned casually, as part of the background of life. A crooked mouse fits quite naturally into the rhyme "There was a crooked man." Rats and mice are pictured as a normal part of the world in:

> *Birds of a feather flock together,*
> *And so will pigs and swine;*
> *The rats and mice will have their choice,*
> *And so will I have mine.*

Sometimes the rhymes show sharp observation of the habits and nature of our ubiquitous houseguests. When the cat who went to London to look at the queen is asked what she did there, we are not at all surprised when she answers, "I frightened a little mouse under the chair." We might have known there would be a mouse hiding there!

The familiar rhyme,

> *Hickory, Dickory, Dock!*
> *The mouse ran up the clock;*
> *The clock struck one,*
> *And down he run,*
> *Hickory, Dickory, Dock!*

sounds just like typical mouse behavior. A mouse is apt to be out exploring its surroundings when no one else is about, and especially at odd hours like one in the morning. Then, timid, it will quickly run away at any frightening loud noise or sudden movement.

One of the most famous jingles in the English language is "Three Blind Mice":

> *Three blind mice, three blind mice,*
> *See how they run, see how they run!*
> *They all ran after the farmer's wife,*
> *Who cut off their tails with a carving knife . . .*
> *Did you ever see such a sight in your life*
> *As three blind mice?*

Some scholars have tried to link this rhyme with history, saying that the "farmer's wife" is really Queen Mary I, who ruled England in the sixteenth century, and the mice are three men that she had put to death. Most people are unaware of this historical association and simply take the rhyme at face value. Mice *do* run about in the kitchen and pantry,

*Mice make pests of themselves in modern kitchens, too.*

and housewives often do fear and hate them; after finding their food gnawed and dirtied, they might well feel like going after the thieving mice with a carving knife.

When Lewis Carroll shrank Alice down for her adventure in Wonderland, she was just about the size of a mouse.

*Alice met a dormouse at the Mad Hatter's tea party.*

Sure enough, her guide at first *was* a mouse, who was terribly upset when Alice was tactless enough to mention her cat. Later Alice met a dormouse at the Mad Hatter's tea party. The poor creature kept falling asleep at the table, and when Alice last saw it, the Mad Hatter and March Hare were trying to stuff it into the teapot.

In weaving mice into his story, Lewis Carroll was continuing a long tradition. Mice are a part of the background in some of the most familiar fairy tales. Do you remember the beautiful coach in which Cinderella went to the ball? Her fairy godmother had made this from a pumpkin. Then she sent Cinderella to find six mice, which she turned into six prancing horses.

In another familiar tale, "Dick Whittington and His Cat," it was a plague of rats and mice that permitted the young hero to make his fortune.

MYTHS AND SUPERSTITIONS

Mice have also played important roles in legends and superstitions far older than fairy tales and Mother Goose rhymes. Strangely, mice have been considered symbols of both good and bad luck by different peoples at different times.

The ancient Greeks noticed that when people were healthy and prosperous, with plenty of food stored away, the numbers of mice increased. So they bred mice in their temples and considered it an omen of good fortune when the mice multiplied rapidly. They linked mice with the sun god Apollo, who was also the patron god of physicians, and thought mice could cure various ills, including constipation, baldness, cataracts, epilepsy, and even snakebite.

Apollo Smintheus, or "Mouse Apollo," was one of the gods worshipped by the Cretans. In about 400 B.C., the Cretans built a temple to this mouse-god on the island of Tenedos in the Aegean Sea. The temple contained a statue of Apollo with a mouse at his feet—and countless numbers of living mice, raised in honor of the god. These sacred mice were of a special variety: their fur was pure white. The statue and temple became famous, and mouse worship spread. People in various parts of the world continued to worship mice until the 1400s.

A legend says that mice also showed the Cretans where to found the famous city of Troy. No one is sure whether the Cretans or some other people really founded Troy, but the legend is an interesting one. Cretan emigrants to Asia Minor, the story goes, had been advised to settle wherever they were attacked by enemies under cover of darkness. It was a time of famine, and one night a horde of starving mice rushed into the Cretan camp and gnawed on the leather straps of the men's shields. This was taken as the sign the men had been waiting for, and they founded Troy nearby.

The Japanese have a traditional belief that the mouse is

a messenger of the god of wealth, who is typically pictured with two sacks of rice and a white mouse. The Chinese raised white mice and used them in their temples to try to foretell the future. They also apparently raised other unusual strains of mice for pets, as did many peoples of the ancient world. In fact, a special word for "spotted mice" appears in a Chinese dictionary written around 1100 B.C.

In Europe during the Middle Ages, there were no doubts at all about whether mice were good or bad. They were regarded as creatures of witches and the Devil, both of whom could supposedly change into mice. It is easy to see why the superstitious thought a witch would want to change into a mouse. As a tiny mouse, a witch could sneak about quietly, listening in on conversations and prying into other people's affairs. (Of course, the witch might want to change back again quickly if there were a cat about!)

Even today, some people are superstitious about mice. They think mice will leave a house where someone is about to die, or one that is going to collapse.

## MOUSE HEROES AND HEROINES

Despite the mouse's reputation for sly sneaking about,

there has always been a countercurrent of sympathy for this shy, delicate animal that is constantly at the mercy of larger creatures. And so, in some tales, the mouse is portrayed as a hero—someone who can help, or outwit, or defeat larger creatures. Young and old alike love stories in which mice, in spite of their tiny size, can be genuine "good guys." The small and weak of the human world can sympathize when story book mice suffer misfortunes and glory in tales of their unexpected triumphs.

Many popular folk songs are based on versions of the rhyme "A Frog Went A-Courtin'." They are sung with a number of different refrains. One version begins:

*There was a frog liv'd in a well,*
*And a merry mouse in a mill.*

*This frog he would a-wooing ride,*
*And on a snail he got astride.*

*He rode till he came to my Lady Mouse hall*
*And there he did both knock and call.*

*Quoth he, "Miss Mouse, I'm come to thee,*
*So see if thou can fancy me."*

*Quoth she, "Answer I'll give you none,
Until my Uncle Rat come home."*

*A Frog Went a-Courtin'.*

As the story continues, Uncle Rat gives his permission for the mouse and frog to wed. The end varies with the different versions. In one, the unlucky frog is swallowed by a duck on his way home from visiting Miss Mouse. In other versions, a grand wedding is held, and many different animals and insects attend.

This fantasy is a love story of the little folk of the world. The versions with unhappy endings show how people's hopes and plans can be destroyed by forces beyond their control. The triumphant endings of other versions of the tale offer a bit of hope for the weak of the world.

The folktales relating the love story of the frog and the mouse are hundreds of years old, but the story itself actually dates back much further. An ancient Greek satire called "The War of Frogs and Mice" was a humorous retelling of the *Iliad*, the great epic about the Trojan War. In the satire, the frog king Physiognathos kidnaps the mouse princess Aricharpax, and the frog and mouse kingdoms go to war. Each ruler calls upon his gods, who help in the fight, and the terrible war lasts a whole day.

Mouse stories continue to delight young and old. Some stories give a mouse-eye view of events in the human world. When we were children, we were amused by the tale of a mouse who lived in Benjamin Franklin's desk and witnessed the American colonists' struggle for independence from England. It seemed a fitting continuation of the tradition when our children brought home a book about Sammy the White House Mouse.

*Stuart Little,* the classic children's story by E. B. White, tells of the many adventures of the mouse Stuart, who has a human brother and human parents. In the popular Basil of Baker Street books by Eve Titus, Basil is a famous English mouse detective.

Mouse heroes have always been featured in cartoons and comic books. There is Mighty Mouse, the Superman of the mouse world. And millions of children and adults are familiar with Tom and Jerry, the cat and mouse antagonists. (In Tom and Jerry cartoons, the little mouse, Jerry, always manages to have the last laugh.) But perhaps the most famous of all cartoon mice is Walt Disney's Mickey Mouse, who has been around since 1928 and is known all over the world.

*Probably the most famous mouse in the world is Walt Disney's Mickey Mouse.*

# CHAMPIONS AT SURVIVAL

Now, perhaps more than ever before, the living things of our world are faced with a very serious problem: they must adapt or perish. Only those animals and plants that can change their ways and adapt to new conditions can survive when their environment changes. Humans have been bringing changes to the world on a vast scale and at a very rapid pace.

In the past centuries, we have explored our world and settled new lands. Cities have grown up where there was only wilderness before. The spread of human civilization across the earth has had far-reaching effects. Humans have cleared forests and fields to plant their crops. They have bulldozed miles and miles of land to lay highways, and the roads with their swiftly moving vehicles form dangerous barriers to the creatures living near them. Humans have filled in swamps, and have built dams that have flooded vast regions of land. With the shrinking of the wilderness, many kinds of creatures have vanished from the earth. Humans also kill animals for food and sport, and exterminate those they consider pests.

## ADAPT OR PERISH

Many creatures cannot change their ways easily. Most of the animals that live in the jungles of Africa and South America could not survive even a mild winter in the northern United States. (Scientists believe that one of the reasons the great dinosaurs died out was that they could not get used to the colder winters that came with the Ice ages in the distant past.) Some animals can eat only certain foods, and if they do not have them they will die. The koala bears from Australia, for example, can eat only eucalyptus leaves, and any zoo that wants to keep them must provide this special food.

As humans continue to change the world, more and more kinds of animals and plants face the problem of adapting or vanishing forever. Less than two hundred years ago, billions of passenger pigeons roosted in the woodlands of our country and darkened the skies like a great moving cloud during their migrations each year. Now they are gone. There is not a single passenger pigeon left alive in the whole world.

Others, too, have lost the fight for the survival of their kind. The dodo and the great auk are gone. And fur seals almost disappeared because they could not change their ways. Each year they flocked back to the same mating grounds, where hunters waited with harpoons, clubs, and guns. Fur seals have been saved only because humans have passed strict laws to protect them.

Hundreds of kinds of animals are now at the edge of extinction. They may disappear, just as the passenger pigeon did, if steps are not taken to save them.

Though some animals have been unable to change, others have proved to be champions at survival. We humans are probably the most adaptable animals of all. We have learned to live in all parts of the world, from the frozen wastes of the Arctic to the steaming jungles of the tropics. We can eat a wide variety of foods, from roasted ants to beefsteaks, from coconuts to corn on the cob. We have even been able, to some extent, to adapt our environment to suit our own needs. We build shelters and wear clothing to keep out the cold and rain. We grow foods that came originally from distant lands and have even learned to grow some foods out of season. We have trained animals and invented machines to work for us.

Yet everywhere that humans have gone, and survived, our resourceful rodent commensals have gone too. *Mus musculus* and its larger relatives, the house rats, have been able to change their habits readily and to survive in many different kinds of surroundings. (Rats and mice now make up the entire wild mammal population of Antarctica!) Their wild ancestors lived in forests and fields, feeding on grains, fruits, smaller animals, and insects. House mice and rats today can live that way too, and in rural areas they may move out for the summer, to live off the land and enjoy a bountiful harvest of seeds and grains. But it is their ability to share the homes of humans, enjoying the shelter and food that we provide, that has made them so numerous and widespread today.

*Two white-footed mice at home in the wild.*

## MUS MUSCULUS AT HOME

The ancestors of the house mouse were burrowing animals. Today there are still wild strains of *Mus musculus* in the Old World that live in branching complexes of tunnels, dug out in the soil of fields where plant cover and food are readily available. Each family of mice has its own nest, lined with soft grasses, feathers, and fibers that block off drafts and help to keep the nest warm, humid, and cozy. A male mouse lives there with his mate (or sometimes two mates) and young family. Tunnels connect the nest with other nests and with community eating places, storage burrows, areas for urination and defecation, and escape holes. There is a great deal of visiting back and forth among members of a mouse community, and they often get together for grooming sessions, picking parasites such as lice and fleas out of each other's fur and getting to know each other better.

Males in the mouse community fight to establish their place in the social structure and to win the right to a nest and a mate. Females do not take part in this fighting for dominance in the community, but a female raising a litter may fight fiercely to defend her babies against intruders. All the mice in a community defend their home territory against mice from other burrows, launching a biting, rushing

*Sniffing and grooming are important parts of a mouse's life.*

attack that usually sends the stranger scampering off.

It is dark inside a mouse burrow, and the mice that live there find their way about by smell. Special glands on the soles of a mouse's feet produce an oily substance that marks off an odor trail as the mouse patters along. Mice follow these odor trails—their own and those of other community members—as they move about the burrows and search for food. The boundaries of the community's territory are carefully marked with urine. To a mouse's sensitive nose, the scents in the urine markers act as chemical "no trespassing" signs that warn strange mice to stay away.

Members of a community recognize one another by smell. Researchers have found that if a "strange" mouse is rubbed with materials from a burrow and then introduced into that burrow, the mice of the community will accept the newcomer readily, not realizing that he or she does not belong.

Female mice can mate when they are about two months old. In cold regions, they have litters only during the warmer months of the year, when the temperature is above about 50° Fahrenheit (10°C). But in hot regions they may have young all year round. The babies—usually five to eight of them—are born just three weeks after mating. They are tiny, hairless, blind, and completely helpless. Their mother feeds them with her milk, and the father mouse helps to clean and care for them. If the nest is threatened, the mother mouse may try to move her young to a safer place, nudging them with her nose and paws or carrying them carefully in her mouth, one by one.

The young mice mature quickly. By the time they are

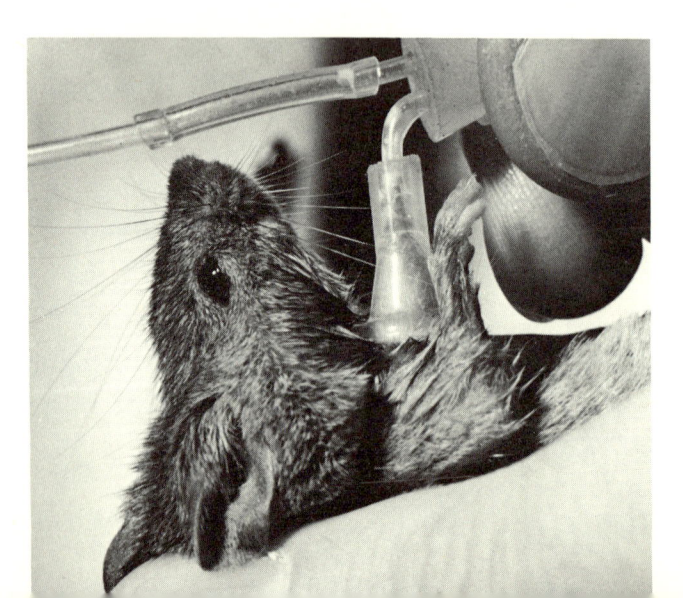

*This mother mouse's milk is being collected for study with a suction device.*

three weeks old, they are eating solid food and ready to be weaned, and in another week or so they are ready to leave the nest. Their parents take them out on trips, showing them around the territory. If the burrow is getting crowded, the mother mouse may take her offspring outside and drop them off in a good place for digging a new burrow.

*Mus musculus* in the wild is mainly a seed-eater, gathering seeds that have fallen to the ground, or sometimes climbing up to pick them off plants. Insects are another ready source of food. Surprisingly, house mice can get along without a source of water to drink, especially if they are living on seeds and grains. Grains might seem like a very dry food, but actually they contain about 10 percent water by weight. In addition, their solid matter is mainly starchy carbohydrate, and when this food material is digested by a mouse's body, more water is produced. (Digesting protein and fat, on the other hand, is a process that uses up water, and more water is required to flush the waste products of proteins out of the body.) The body fluids of insects also provide some water, and in dry times up to 90 percent of a mouse's diet may be made up of insects.

*Mus musculus* is much better equipped than we are for saving water. In dry times, this tiny rodent's kidneys can produce a very concentrated urine—it may be up to four times as salty as seawater. (In fact, mice living in coastal regions drink seawater without harm. Humans cannot do this.) Even a nursing mother mouse does not lose as much water as one might expect. Her milk contains a lower percentage of water than that of most other mammals, and it is often as fatty as the milk of whales, which have the richest milk of all the mammals.

When conditions are really dry, a mouse may lose up to 40 percent of its body weight in water and still recover quickly when water is available again. If its body water level falls too low, it has a last resort—"sleeping it out." The mouse goes into a sort of hibernating state; its body temperature falls, and its breathing, heartbeat, and all its body reactions slow down. In this unconscious state, the mouse's body reserves are used up much more slowly than usual. After a few days (or sooner, if it is disturbed), the mouse wakes up and goes out to see if things have improved.

Mice in the wild have many enemies. Owls and hawks swoop down to catch them as they scurry about gathering seeds. Snakes may actually slither right into their burrows to catch them. Hunting animals—from tiny shrews and lizards to cats, dogs, and foxes—prey on mice. Even predators as large as mountain lions may fill their bellies entirely with mice.

Against all these enemies, the mouse has just one main line of defense—its natural timidity. It stays under cover and close to shelter as much as it can. Even when its curiosity drives it to explore new surroundings, a mouse is constantly on the alert for danger. A threatening noise or an alarming smell will send it immediately scooting or leaping for safety. (A mouse's small size helps it here—it can squeeze into tiny holes and cracks to escape predators.) A cornered mouse will fight with teeth and claws, especially if it is a mother defending her young—the mouse may even turn and rise on its haunches in a fighting posture to confront a cat. But the first instinct of a mouse in danger is to run away.

Because they are relatively defenseless, many mice are killed by predators. Many others die of disease. But mice have one very powerful weapon for survival: their amazing ability to multiply. Under ideal conditions, a female mouse can have a litter of as many as a dozen or more every three weeks, for she is ready to mate again as soon as her young are born. If her mate is killed, she will soon accept another; indeed, the smell of a strange male mouse can make a group of females all ready to mate immediately, even if some of them were in a part of their normal sexual cycle when they would not have been interested in mating. When you consider that each of the young mice in a litter will, in turn, be ready to mate and produce litters of its own within about two months, it is easy to calculate that just a few generations of ideal breeding would quickly enlarge a mouse population by thousands.

Usually predators, food supply, and other natural factors keep mouse populations pretty well under control. If their territory gets too crowded, the male mice become more quarrelsome than usual. Fights for dominance are more frequent, and the top male may not permit any of the others in the community to mate. Under crowded conditions, many of the female mice may become infertile—changes in their bodies make them unable to bear young. Soon a more normal population level is restored.

Occasionally, though, mouse populations build up to huge numbers before natural factors can bring them back under control. Mouse plagues, involving *Mus musculus* and other species, have been reported in various parts of the world. In 1926–27, for example, house mice and meadow mice suddenly began to multiply wildly in the bed of a California lake that had been drained to plant crops. The mice ate up every available bit of food on the lake bed—they gnawed grass, corn, and other plants right down to the roots, and consumed ninety-one sacks of barley seed that had been sown on the fields. Then they swarmed outward, traveling as much as ten miles in a night and invading houses, barns, and other buildings in their path. Anxious ranchers counted seventeen mice to a square yard, or eighty-two thousand to an acre. Owls, hawks, gulls, coyotes, and other predators came in to feast on the swarming mice, and ranchers poisoned cartloads full of rodents before the plague died down.

## THE COMMENSAL LIFE

Mice that moved from the fields into people's buildings found protection from many of their natural enemies and a much richer and more dependable source of food. Their natural habits and skills fitted them well to life with humans. Spaces between walls and under floorboards were ideal for their nests and runways. Bits of paper, cloth, stuffing from furniture, and other soft materials pilfered from various places around the house made an ideal nest lining. Food was readily available to an animal that could scamper up walls, jump up on shelves, and gnaw through boxes and bags. Drinking water might be more of a problem, but usually the mice could get along without it. (House mice can live and multiply in granaries, which are kept as dry as possible to keep the stored grain from spoiling.) In heated buildings house mice can breed all year round, but mice have also been found thriving in meat refrigerators. There they live on an all-meat diet, grow longer, thicker coats of fur, and gnaw out cozy nests inside the racked meats.

Mice living the commensal life are not completely without enemies. Cats, rats, and barn owls take their toll of house mice. Humans, annoyed by the damage caused by these small thieves, trap and poison them. Even when many individual mice perish, their species goes triumphantly on, for it is almost impossible to wipe out an entire colony of mice. An unwary young mouse caught in a trap may have a dozen brothers and sisters at home in a snug nest in a hollow inside the wall. Even if nearly all the mice in a building are killed, a single pregnant female can soon have the colony reestablished.

## COUNTRY COUSINS

If house mice have been spectacularly successful at living with humans, their country cousins have been equally good at surviving in their own ways. Over a thousand species of mice and rats live wild, and they have adapted very well indeed to their widely varied environments.

Like *Mus musculus*, wild mice can breed often and produce many offspring at a time. A wild mouse's young, like human children in the same family, may vary considerably. One young mouse may be able to tolerate hotter temperatures than another; one may be better able to live on a particular kind of food; one may have fur of a color that hides it better from its enemies. With so many young born at a time, growing so quickly and soon producing many young of their own, there is a good chance that at least some of each new generation will be well adapted to survive in new territories, or under conditions that previous generations could not tolerate. The mice best fitted for life in a particular region are those with the best chance of surviving there. Often they pass on to their own young the characteristics that have helped them to survive. Thus the mice of a particular region may gradually become better and better adapted to their environment.

To small rodents that live the difficult and dangerous life of the hunted, any slight advantage that helps them to keep from being eaten by predators can mean the difference between extinction and the survival of the species. Protective coloration often provides this important advantage. Fur with a color or pattern that blends into the surroundings makes a mouse hard for a predator to see. Mice that live in fields

*Variations of fur color have permitted pocket mice to blend with their surroundings in different habitats.*

or run about on the brown forest floor often have dull-colored, brownish coats. Those that live in deserts or on sandy beaches have pale, sandy-colored fur. Commensals typically have darker fur than their wild relatives, the better to hide unnoticed in shadowy corners.

Near the White Sands National Monument in New Mexico, scientists have observed an amazing example of color adaptability. At White Sands there are white pocket mice whose pale fur makes them almost invisible against the white sand dunes. Only a few miles away, the ground is covered with black lava—a volcano once erupted there. On this black rock live pocket mice very closely related to those at White Sands, and very much like them in every respect but one—their fur is dark. In the hills nearby the soil is reddish, and here still a third variety of pocket mice is found. These mice have reddish fur that matches the soil on which they live.

Adaptation such as this does not happen all at once. It is a process that may take hundreds or thousands of generations. A mouse living in the white-sand area may have had litters including both dark and light babies. The darker mice were easier for predators to spot and catch. More of them were killed, while more of their lighter brothers and sisters survived to have offspring of their own. This process went on until at last only light-furred mice remained. A very similar process occurred on the black lava rock, except that here it was the dark-furred mice that survived and multiplied.

The ability to adapt in various ways to a wide range of living conditions has permitted mice and mouselike rodents to spread literally all over the world. Some of these small rodents are to be found in every country, feeding on seeds or grasses, insects, snails, or other small animals (even mice!), the eggs of birds or reptiles, and any other food that is available. Some mouse species live in grasslands, some in forests. Some thrive in wet marshlands, while others have adapted to the hot, dry desert where there is not a drop of water to be had. All together, their numbers are huge: there are more individual rodents in the world than all the other warm-blooded animals put together.

# IN FOREST, FIELD, AND DESERT

To the average city dweller, the word "mouse" means just one thing: the house mouse, *Mus musculus*. But around the world there are many hundreds of different kinds of mice, as well as a variety of mouselike creatures that are commonly called by other names—for example, voles, rats, lemmings, and hamsters. Members of the mouse families are found in hot, steaming jungles and in even hotter, dry deserts. Mice and their kin live in tree-filled forests and grass-covered meadows, low marshlands and high mountain ranges. Some, like the Old World rats and house mice, are still able to adapt readily to new conditions. Others have adapted so well to the special conditions of their homes that they could not easily survive anywhere else.

It would take much too long (and be rather boring) to try to describe all the species of mice that live in our world. Many of them are so similar that only a scientist could tell them apart. Here, instead, are some facts about a few of the most interesting members of mousedom and the unusual traits that help them to survive in their particular environments.

## AT HOME IN THE DESERT

The kangaroo rats are a group of New World rodents that are only distantly related to other mice and rats. In fact, scientists actually place them in the group of squirrel-like rodents, Sciuromorpha, rather than the "mouse-shaped" Myomorpha. These timid little animals are found only in the desert areas of North America. Like kangaroos, they have very short forelegs and long, strong hind legs with which they can go leaping through the air. Their long tails (usually longer than their bodies) help them to balance and turn nimbly in the air in the middle of a leap.

Kangaroo rats and their smaller cousins, the pocket mice, are amazingly well adapted to life in the desert. They live in individual burrows that are mazes of branching tunnels leading to many storerooms and a nest buried deep inside. These burrows provide them with a place to hide from their enemies, such as coyotes, owls, and snakes. The deep burrows also help kangaroo rats to survive the blazing heat of the desert. There they stay all day, with the entrances to the burrow tightly blocked off with sand. At night they come out to gather food and socialize with other kangaroo rats living in the nearby burrows.

Kangaroo rats and pocket mice gather seeds and pack

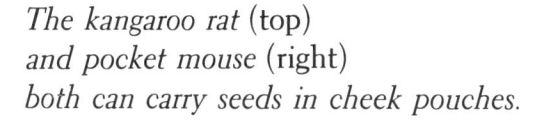

*The kangaroo rat* (top)
*and pocket mouse* (right)
*both can carry seeds in cheek pouches.*

them away in special fur-lined pouches in their cheeks. These are the "pockets" that give pocket mice their name. The pouches can stretch and stretch to hold hundreds or even thousands of tiny seeds. When a kangaroo rat has filled its pouches and its cheeks are bulging out on both sides, it scurries back to its burrow to store away the food it has gathered. Grasses and other nesting materials are also carried in the pouches, which can be turned inside out for cleaning.

The kangaroo rat's seed storehouse not only serves as a source of food, but also helps the animal in another way. During the day, as the kangaroo rat stays in its closed-up burrow, it loses some moisture in its breath and perspiration. The air of the burrow becomes laden with dampness, but the precious droplets of moisture are not lost entirely. They soak into the dry seeds, which the little rodent will later eat. The water contained in these "dry" seeds, and water produced from the food during digestion, provide the kangaroo rat with all the moisture it needs.

The kangaroo rat has some interesting tricks for escaping from its enemies. With its long legs, it can leap away to take refuge in its burrow. It may then suddenly stop short and, with some quick scratching motions, send a spray of loose sand back into the face of its pursuer.

The Old World has its deserts, too, and it also has mouselike rodents in these hot, dry regions. Among these are the gerbils, which recently have become quite popular as pets here in the United States. Gerbils are native to desert areas in Asia and Africa.

Like kangaroo rats, gerbils have long hind legs and hop about, rather than scurrying as most rodents do. They have large ears that help them to hear sounds over great distances across the desert landscape and thus escape from approaching enemies.

Unlike kangaroo rats, gerbils are active mostly during the day. Their sand-colored fur blends with the sandy environ-

*Gerbils in the Old World deserts resemble the New World kangaroo rats.*

ment in which they live and makes them very hard to see.

Gerbils live in burrows, which are sometimes great networks of community tunnels shared by many gerbils. They get all the water they need from the seeds and roots they eat, and do not need to drink water.

Usually gerbils and the other "sand rats" that live in the deserts of Asia and Africa do not annoy humans. The gerbils in India, however, sometimes multiply so fast that they suddenly break out in great swarms, sweeping through the countryside and laying waste fields of grain.

In some desert areas, spiny mice live in gerbil burrows and may compete with them for food. The hairs of the spiny mouse's fur coat are modified into sharp, stiff spines, like the spines of a hedgehog.

*The Malabar spiny mouse.*

The Cairo spiny mouse of Egypt is rather unusual in its breeding behavior. Its young develop inside the mother's body for much longer than the young of most other rodents—thirty-eight days—and when the babies are born, their eyes are open and they have full coats of silky fur. Just before the birth, the mother spiny mouse develops a powerful maternal feeling. She tries to steal one of her neighbor's babies, holds it carefully in her paws to groom it, and may even suckle it. When her own litter is born, she is a careful and conscientious mother. The babies are weaned at two weeks, and are ready to breed when they are only seven weeks old.

Various other species of spiny mice are found in the deserts and woodlands of Asia and Africa, where they feed mainly on seeds and other plant foods. Some live in or near human dwellings, and, like house mice, these spiny mice will eat almost anything. In the Americas there are several species of spiny mice belonging to the vole family, and a number of species of spiny pocket mice, some of them "spinier" than others.

## SHY WOOD DWELLERS

Dainty little white-footed mice can be found almost everywhere in the woodlands of North America. These tiny forest creatures are named for their snow-white feet. Their bellies are also white, but the fur on their backs and heads is usually a dull brown. White-footed mice of some species are also called wood mice because they live in the woodlands; another name often used is deer mice, because their color and markings resemble those of the deer that live in the same forests.

*The white-footed mouse.*

Vesper mice is still another name, used because these mice can often be heard "singing" toward evening. (Special evening church services are called "vespers.") White-footed mice do make a sort of trilling or buzzing sound that is quite different from the typical squeaks of other mice. They also drum with their feet when they are excited.

A white-footed mouse builds its nest in some warm, dry nook—a hollow tree or stump, an abandoned squirrel's nest, or perhaps a burrow. These mice sometimes find their way into vacation homes that are closed for the winter, and build cozy nests in mattresses or bureau drawers. The returning householder may have an unpleasant surprise. Although white-footed mice are extremely clean in their personal habits, constantly groom themselves and keep their fur neat and shining, they are very sloppy housekeepers. They do not bother to leave the nest to urinate and defecate, and they also drop bits of food into their bedding as they eat. Within a week or two, the nest is such a sodden, stinking mess that even the mouse can't stand it, and he or she moves on to make another nest somewhere else.

White-footed mice sometimes make nuisances of themselves by eating crops or seeds that farmers have planted, but mostly they live quietly, away from humans. Constantly on the lookout for such enemies as owls, lynxes, weasels, and foxes, they scurry about in the woods at night, feeding on nuts and seeds that they gather and insects that they catch. They help to protect the forest by eating large numbers of the insect grubs that can damage the roots of young trees.

Red-backed mice, which have bright reddish brown fur on their backs also live in the forests of North America. These mice are busy both night and day, searching the forest

*The Korean red-backed mouse.*

floor, mole burrows, and even the lower branches of trees for nuts, seeds, berries, bark, and insects to eat or store away for the lean times of winter, when food will be harder to find.

Old World woodland mice are very much like those of the New World. Yellow-necked mice scurry about at night and nest in burrows and hollows, like the white-footed mice of North America. And like the wood mice of America, they store plenty of food for winter. The yellow-necked mouse, unlike some Old World species, does not hibernate but is active all year round.

## TREETOP HOMES

Several kinds of mice actually make their homes in trees. Red tree mice are found only in the great forests of spruce and fir in the northwestern United States. They live on the needles and young shoots of fir trees. The females live high up in the trees in large nests built of twigs and needles. The males, however, live on the forest floor or in burrows underground. It is believed that the males and females meet only during the breeding season, when the males climb a few feet up into the trees and build small, makeshift nests, where mating takes place. The males soon go back to the ground, and the females return to their treetop nests to bear and raise their young.

Red tree mice have become so restricted in their way of life, and especially in their diet, that if the particular kinds of trees in which they live were destroyed by disease, fire, or human activities, the mice would perish, too. They could not survive even in a different kind of forest, much less in a meadow, marsh, or desert.

Tree-dwelling mice are also found in central and eastern Asia. Some of these have adapted to their life in the trees in quite unusual ways. The long-tailed tree mouse of central Asia has a tail that can grip things almost like a hand. This tail helps it to hold on to the branches of the trees in which it lives. The marmoset tree mouse of the area formerly known as Indochina has hands almost like a monkey's. With its tiny thumbs and fingers it can easily hold on to small branches or pick up seeds and berries.

The most famous tree-dwelling mouse is the European dormouse, well known to generations of readers of *Alice in Wonderland*. Many different kinds of dormice are found in various parts of Europe, Asia, and Africa. These little rodents are very much like squirrels. They live in trees and feed on nuts, seeds, and fruits; some kinds have long, bushy

*A dormouse with a dreamy expression . . .*

tails. They are favorite pets in many parts of Europe.

The name of the dormouse comes from the French word *dormir*, which means "to sleep." Dormice deserve their name. They have adapted to the changing seasons of their homes by hibernating through the coldest part of the year.

During the summer and early fall, the dormouse busily eats and grows fatter and fatter. Then, when the weather is getting colder and winter is near, it crawls into its winter nest. There it curls up with its tail wrapped around itself and goes to sleep until spring.

Once they start to hibernate, dormice are very hard to awaken. Sometimes they do awaken, though, take a meal from the supply of nuts and seeds they have stored away in the nest, and go back to sleep again.

## IN MEADOWS AND FIELDS

Mice and their kin abound not only in woods and forests, but also in meadows and fields. Small mouselike rodents called voles build great networks of runways and nests in the grass, or sometimes build grass nests and storerooms in underground burrows. Their covered runways help to protect them from their many enemies.

The life of the meadow vole (or meadow mouse or field mouse, as it is also called) is not easy. These small rodents are constantly hungry and are about night and day, searching for seeds, tender grasses and roots, and insects to eat. In the winter they scurry under the snow in search of stray bits of food. They must be constantly alert, for they are hunted in turn. Birds such as hawks, owls, crows, and gulls may swoop down to catch them. Snakes may slither into

*Meadow mice.*

their burrows. Weasels, skunks, bobcats, foxes, and even bears prey upon them. Meadow mice are good swimmers, but in ponds and streams they may be caught and eaten by bullfrogs, trout, and turtles.

Lemmings, which are closely related to voles, live in the Arctic tundra or in fields in cold northern climates. Perhaps you have heard tales of the lemmings of Norway, which periodically pour out of their mountain homes in huge migrations and mindlessly cast themselves into the sea in mass suicide. These stories are rather exaggerated, but, as we have seen, a rodent "population explosion" can result in a mass migration. Every few years, when favorable weather conditions provide an especially large food supply and a long breeding period, the lemmings suddenly begin to have larger litters than usual, and more litters in a year. The lemming population soon outgrows its food supply, and the animals begin emigrating outward in all directions. Many of them die before they can establish new homes, dropping from exhaustion or disease, being trampled, or drowning in rivers and fjords.

One species of lemming is especially well adapted to the climate of its frigid homeland. These animals, the snow lemmings, turn pure white in the winter. As they walk about on the snow and burrow under it, their white fur provides

*The collared lemming.*

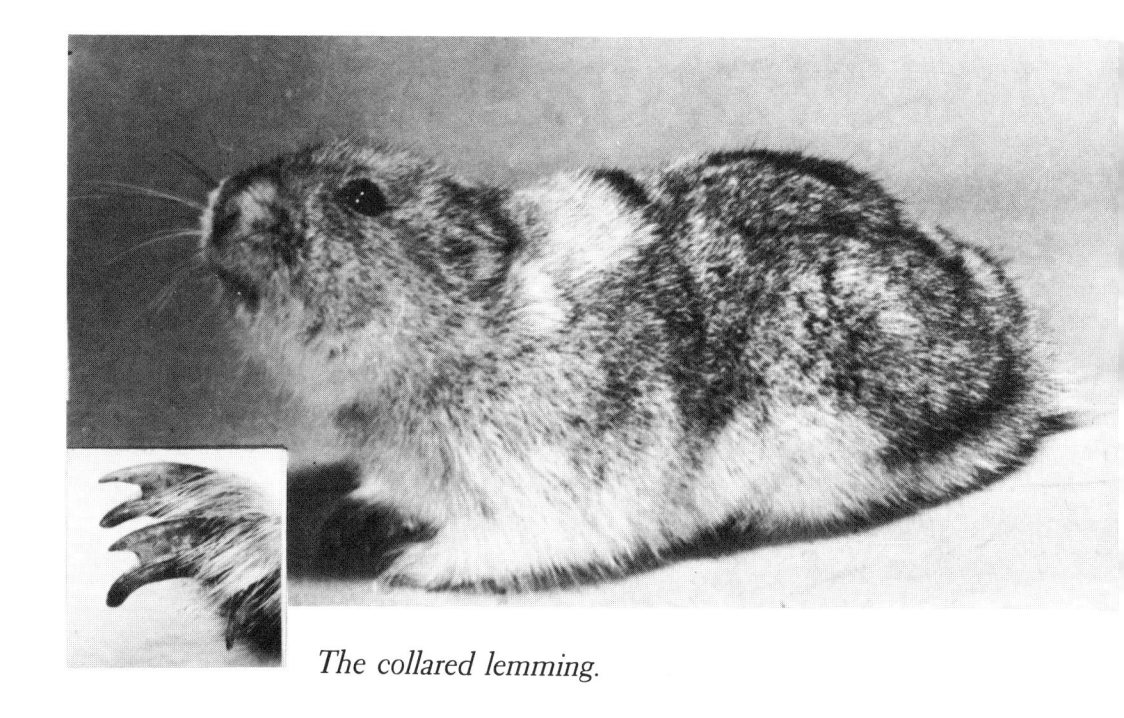

effective camouflage. When the weather turns warm and the snow melts, the snow lemming's white fur is replaced by a darker coat, and the animal is called the collared lemming.

The snow lemming adapts to wintry weather in another way as well. In the fall, it grows large temporary claws under the permanent ones on its third and fourth fingers. These special claws act as snow shovels.

Tiny mice with long, slender tails are found in fields and meadows of both the Old and New worlds. These are the harvest mice. They can scamper up and down long blades of grass and swing back and forth like acrobats, gripping with their tiny feet and even with their tails.

Harvest mice build their nests a foot or more above the ground in tall grasses. They carefully weave grasses into perfect balls; these are firmly attached to growing grass supports and lined with finely shredded grass and leaves. Inside, the babies are born and grow, in their snug round cradles rocked by the swaying grasses.

*The eastern harvest mouse: note the clinging tail.*

*The pine mouse looks rather like a mole.*

The pine mouse, a field and meadow mouse of Europe, Asia, and the eastern United States, is also sometimes found in woodlands. It got its name from the fact that it was first seen in the pine forests of Georgia.

The pine mouse is very much like a mole in many ways, well adapted to a life underground. It has very small eyes and ears, a stubby tail, and short velvety fur that lies smooth when brushed either forward or back—the perfect coat for an animal that spends its time scrambling backward and forward in underground burrows and tunnels.

Like moles, pine mice are great pests to farmers. They dig long tunnels in the soil, feeding on tubers and roots, and sometimes venture above ground to gather seeds or berries. Pine mice can ruin a field of potatoes or damage orchard trees by gnawing their roots.

## BUILT FOR SPEED

Strange little creatures called jumping mice, or kangaroo mice, can be found living under a variety of conditions in many different parts of the United States and Canada—in meadows and marshes, woodlands, and dry, sandy areas. Jumping mice all have tiny forelegs, large hind legs, and unusually long tails that help them to balance as they go

*The woodland jumping mouse.*

leaping about like tiny kangaroos. (They are not very closely related to kangaroo rats, however, and are classified in a different family from most of the other mice.) The tiny jumping mice, with bodies only about three inches long, can go up to ten or twelve feet in one hop.

The meadow jumping mouse feeds on seeds, flowers, and insects. If it lives in a wet, marshy area, it may build its nest in tall grasses or bushes where it can stay dry.

Woodland jumping mice usually live in burrows, which they dig close to a source of water. They eat mainly seeds, but when the berries are in season they will climb up into bushes to get them; often their dainty white feet and bellies become stained with the dribbling berry juices. During the mating season, these jumping mice come out of their burrows on moonlit nights to do a curious sort of dance, jumping up and down like rubber balls on strings. In the wintertime, they are not to be found. They are curled up, fast asleep, in their cozy fur-lined burrows, hibernating until spring.

Another family of mouselike jumping rodents, the jerboas, is found in desert regions of Europe, Asia, and North Africa. The jerboa has long, soft, silky fur, a dark mask across its face, and a tuft of fur at the tip of its long tail. Jerboas

*The desert jerboa is built for speed.*

live in large communal burrows, and come out in swarms after the infrequent desert rains to feast on the insects and vegetation that spring up overnight as soon as moisture is available. Pictures of jerboas have been found in ancient Egyptian temples and tombs, and their long-legged shape was simplified into a hieroglyphic symbol meaning "swiftness."

## BOLD HUNTERS OF THE RODENT WORLD

Grasshopper mice, found in the western United States, are quite unmouselike. They live not as timid seed-gatherers, but as bold hunters. They are called grasshopper mice because of their fondness for insects such as grasshoppers. They may also kill and eat various kinds of mice and can dig up insects hiding in the ground. They sometimes eat seeds and

*The grasshopper mouse.*

grasses, too, but they feed mainly on insects and other small animals, so they are quite helpful to humans.

A grasshopper mouse hunts at night and goes after its prey like a miniature hunting dog. It creeps silently along on padded feet, sniffing the ground for a likely scent. When it is on a trail it becomes excited and follows the scent eagerly, wagging its short tail and squeaking sharply. When its prey is in sight, it is upon it with a leap and kills it with its long, sharp front teeth.

Grasshopper mice adapt easily to captivity, and they make surprisingly gentle pets. They can be useful pets, too—if they are allowed the run of the house, their nightly forays will keep it free of cockroaches and other insect pests.

## MARSUPIAL MICE

There is one group of mice that are not rodents. These are the marsupial mice of Australia, tiny relatives of the kangaroo. Unlike rodents, marsupial mice have a full set of teeth, with eight incisors in the top jaw and six in the bottom, as well as pointed canines and various grinding teeth. Like kangaroos and the other marsupial animals of Australia, marsupial mice carry their young in a pouch. The babies

*The row of tiny pointed teeth in the mouth of this marsupial mouse reveals that it is not a rodent.*

stay in the pouch, tightly attached to their mother's teats, for about a month, until they are well developed enough to venture out on their own.

Marsupial mice are not timid seed-eaters; they are fierce hunters, feeding on insects such as beetles, roaches, and termites, as well as on centipedes, spiders, small lizards, and house mice. In turn, they are preyed on by cats, snakes, owls, and other hunting animals.

# THE BALANCE OF NATURE

History researchers, reading through old Italian court records, discovered a description of a rather curious lawsuit. In 1519 the farmers around Stelvio, in northern Italy, charged that the field mice of the area had severely damaged their crops. The mice did not appear in court to defend themselves, but an able lawyer was appointed to plead their case. The defense attorney argued that the mice had actually helped the farmers of the region by killing destructive insects and grubs, and by stirring up and enriching the soil.

However, since the damage charged was proved conclusively, the judge sentenced all the mice to immediate exile from the area. Taking their good character references into consideration, he also ordered that the exiles be provided safe conduct on their way out. Farmers and townspeople were to keep their dogs and cats in check, and they even were ordered to build bridges over small streams so that the mice could cross. Mice who were old or with young were given an additional fourteen days to leave. Unfortunately, the records do not say whether the court of Stelvio was ever able to enforce its decrees.

## THE DELICATE BALANCE

The world of nature is in a fine and delicate balance. Plants grow when they have enough sunlight, water, warmth, and space. Animals, from tiny insects to huge elephants, feed upon them. And, of course, many animals (including humans) kill and feed upon other animals.

All the animals and plants of our planet are dependent upon one another. Animals that eat plants can grow and multiply only as long as there are enough plants for them to eat, and enough plants remaining to provide growth for the future. Animals that feed on other animals can grow and multiply only as long as there are enough of their prey for them to feed on. If they caught and ate *all* the prey animals in an area, there would be none left to breed and multiply, and the predators would soon starve.

Mice are such small creatures that you might not think they could be very important in nature. Yet these small rodents are among the most important forms of life in the forests, fields, and deserts of the world. They may be tiny, but there are enormous numbers of them. In a given area there are usually more mice than any other kinds of mammals. Mice are the largest source of food for a great variety of animals, from hunting birds (such as hawks and owls)

*Nature's hunters, such as this great horned owl, help keep mouse populations in control.*

to predatory mammals (such as foxes, coyotes, skunks, martens, and wildcats) to reptiles (such as snakes).

Almost every community of nature has its own mice. As we saw in the last chapter, some can live only under very special conditions—for example, the red tree mice found only in spruce and fir forests. Others, such as field mice, are spread throughout most of the world.

Wherever there are mice, the same pattern is repeated. These small rodents seem to be everyone's prey. Predators, both large and small, find these tiny, defenseless creatures to be perfect meals. But the surviving mice breed rapidly, so the species does not die out and the predators rarely go hungry. This has gone on for countless generations of both mice and predators.

## MAN INTERFERES

The resources of nature are so delicately balanced that it is not surprising that even small changes can have far-reaching results. Humans have made and are making many such changes, sometimes unthinkingly. Often the results are beyond their wildest dreams—or nightmares.

Not long ago, farmers in Yugoslavia watched helplessly

as hordes of field mice swept through their fields, leaving devastation in their wake. For nearly two hundred miles, nothing edible was safe. The small, yellow-furred invaders cut down corn, rye, and wheat standing in the fields. They gobbled down beans and tomatoes, and even dug up shallowly planted potatoes.

As the swarms of mice foraged on through the countryside, they spread disease. Hundreds of people came down with hemorrhagic fever, and some died.

What made the situation even worse was that the farmers had only themselves to blame for their troubles. They had just completed a successful campaign to wipe out all the foxes and martens in the area. That had seemed a sensible thing to do: the foxes and martens had been raiding the farmers' chicken coops and attacking their farm animals. But when the foxes and martens were gone, the farmers discovered that they had been eating more field mice than chickens. With their natural enemies gone, the field mice bred and multiplied, bred and multiplied some more. Only a lack of food could limit their population increase. And when food became scarce, the hordes of field mice spread out, looking for more. Soon they were far worse pests than the predators had ever been.

Sometimes people have accidentally brought new kinds

of mice and rats with them when they have settled new lands. Sometimes these new rodents have proved to be better adapted than the native kinds, and they have bred so fast that predators have not been able to keep them under control. Then they have caused destruction, as the mice in Yugoslavia did. Humans have not been the only ones to suffer, either. The number of native wild birds in an area often dwindles as rats move in, because the rodents are so fond of birds' eggs and young.

At times people have tried to undo the damage they have done by attempting to set up new balances among living things. Thus, concerned about the damage rat immigrants to the West Indies were doing to the native wildlife, well-meaning people brought in a famous rat hunter, the mongoose. Unfortunately, the mongooses found the West Indian birds, small mammals, and reptiles even better prey than rats, and soon they were doing more damage than the rats they had been brought in to kill.

## NOT ALL VILLAINS

It is true that mice are sometimes pests, and it is no wonder that people have sometimes tried to exterminate them. But mice are not always villains. As we have seen, they are an important source of food for many animals, including valuable fur animals. Killing off a mouse population usually brings bad results.

When mice disappear from an area, the animals that prey on them begin to feel the pinch of hunger. Many of them starve; others are driven by their hunger into other areas, and they upset the delicate balance among plants and animals there. Thus, the disappearance of a mouse population causes ripples of change, like the ripples that spread out in a pool when a stone is dropped in.

Mice are not only *not* all bad; they are sometimes quite helpful to humans. The clever Italian lawyer who pleaded their case in 1519 was quite truthful when he claimed that field mice kill many destructive insect pests, such as beetles and caterpillars. Wood rats and white-footed mice perform the same sort of service in the forests, and keep many valuable trees from being destroyed by insects. Naturalists have noticed, for example, that white-footed mice are particularly fond of moths and caterpillars. They believe that such mice, prowling about on the undersides of tree branches and in the underbrush, probably catch many insects as they rest there. These insects might be missed by birds because they are not moving about.

Even "Public Enemy Number One," the house rat, and its smaller but equally destructive cousin, the house mouse, have a few good points. As they forage in houses and storerooms, they often kill cockroaches and other vermin that spread filth and disease.

ECOLOGY

Since the 1960s, people have become very conscious of ecology, the branch of science that studies the complex interrelationships of our planet Earth and all its creatures. Laws aimed at protecting the environment have been passed—not only so that we humans will have cleaner air to breathe and purer water to drink, but also to help the varied animals and plants of our world to survive. Scientists have drawn up lists of endangered species—animals and plants whose populations are so small that even a slight change in living conditions might tip the balance toward extinction. Before any major project, such as a dam or a new industrial complex, is begun, scientists must study the area and draw up detailed "environmental impact statements" predicting how the new construction will affect the wildlife (and people) of the region.

Sometimes the interests of wildlife conflict with those

of humans, sparking controversies that are both comic and tragic. One of the most recent involved a little brown mouse that lives in the San Francisco Bay marshes, drinking salt water and feeding on picklewood. This mouse is the salt marsh harvest mouse, officially classified as an endangered species. Colonies of salt marsh harvest mice live right in the middle of one of the sites that a large utility company was considering for a $1.5 billion power plant. Government agencies pondered the problem. A representative of the U.S. Fish and Wildlife Service suggested that the only way to build the power plant on that site without threatening this mouse species would be to build a new marsh just like the old one, live-trap the mice and move them there, and then run studies over many generations to make sure the mice were thriving in their new home—a project that could take

*The salt marsh harvest mouse, an endangered species, was found living at a site being considered for a power plant.*

ten years. Only if the project was a success could the power plant be allowed to be built.

Some people think that the concern over endangered species has gone too far, and that the pressing needs of humanity should come first. With one "energy crisis" after another threatening our way of life, can we afford to wait ten years to build a needed power plant just to save one insignificant species of mouse? Are the costs of all these environmental impact studies and court battles really worth it? In the history of our planet, species after species has become extinct; why should we be so concerned now about losing the snail darter or the long-toed salamander or the salt marsh harvest mouse?

The problem is that we don't yet know enough to be sure. The varied animals and plants of our world are so complexly and delicately interrelated that the loss of one species can have unpredictable effects on others. The results of our meddling—wiping out "pests," moving animals from one continent to another—have often turned out to create further problems. Salt marsh harvest mice blocking the construction of a power plant, field mice eating up farmers' seeds and crops, house mice foraging in the kitchen at night—all these might seem insignificant and easily spared. But if they were lost, what would be the total effect on the complex web of life?

## THE FINAL VICTORY?

It might be interesting to speculate on what would happen if people managed to wipe out *all* the rats and mice in the world.

At first it might seem that the results were good. In the cities, damage due to the rodents' gnawing and their fouling of food supplies would be eliminated, and so would an important cause of the spread of disease. Outside the cities, damage to crops by rats and mice would also cease.

Then the tide would begin to turn. Without rats and mice to help keep them in check, the multitudes of insects that infest forests, fields, and storehouses would multiply. The destruction they cause would increase.

In the communities of nature, the elimination of a major group of food animals would also have far-reaching effects. Predators—hawks and owls, foxes and martens, snakes and even alligators—would begin to feel the pinch of hunger. Many would starve to death. Those that survived would have to range farther and farther afield to find their prey.

Prey animals, too, would feel the effects. With no rats and mice to fill the predators' bellies, rabbits and wildfowl would be hunted more intensively. Soon their populations, too, would begin to fall, and in some areas they would be wiped out entirely. With the killing of more birds and small insect-eating animals, insect populations would skyrocket.

With prey harder and harder to find, the hunters of the wild would grow bolder. Desperate raids on chicken coops and sheep pens would become more and more frequent.

Eventually, of course, nature would reach a new balance. But without rats and mice, our world might be far different, and poorer in living resources than it is now.

# MICE AS PETS

The city of Melbourne, Australia, had mouse problems. People were coming down with food poisoning, and important documents in the Supreme Court building were being nibbled by mice. City health officials thought they had the answer: an all-out war on the city's mice. Traps and poisons would be used, and a law was proposed making it illegal to keep even one pet mouse. The city's chief health officer remarked, "The pet mice breed like the rest and will mate with wild mice if they get the chance." The mouse lovers of Melbourne were outraged. The Australian National Mouse Club began a publicity campaign to convince the city lawmakers that pet mice are actually harmless creatures, clean, healthy, friendly—model citizens, in fact.

People have enjoyed raising pet mice for thousands of years. Mice are attractive little creatures. They don't take up much room, will eat almost anything, and do not require much care. They can become very tame and friendly, and can even learn some tricks. Mice are also just about the least expensive pets you can buy.

The mice that are sold in pet shops today come from

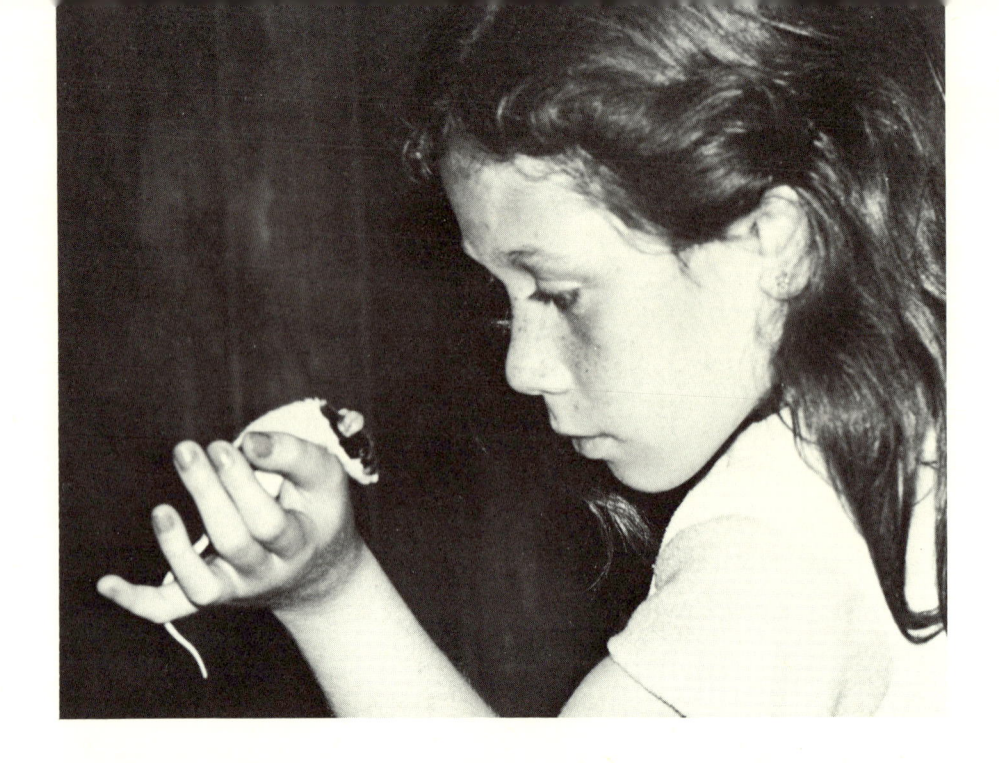

family lines that have been carefully bred for many thousands of generations. By selecting animals that show variations from the original wild ancestors, mouse breeders have developed strains of mice with interesting and unusual colors, as well as a gentle, easily tamed disposition.

There are only two things wrong with mice as pets. The first is their distinctive mousy odor, a sort of musky smell that reminds you of the animal houses at the zoo. The odor comes from the mouse's urine, and it is the cage, rather than the mouse itself, that smells. Feeding pet mice a diet of mainly dry seeds and grains will help to keep the amount of urine and smelly nitrogen wastes down somewhat. But male mice will still scent-mark the boundaries of their territory with urine. Cleaning the cage frequently and keeping the bottom well covered with pleasant-smelling wood shavings is a help—though researchers in one laboratory reported the discouraging finding that the more often they cleaned the cages, the more frequently their mice urinated all over them. Apparently they were determined to replace their scent markers as promptly as possible. If members of your family find a mousy smell objectionable, the only thing to do is to keep the cage in a room where the smell will not bother anyone, or to keep only female mice, which do not engage in territorial marking and so do not urinate as much.

The other problem with mouse pets is that if one gets loose, you have a mouse in the house, and it may become a pest. The danger of escapes is greatest when mice are new, before they have had a chance to become tame and get used to their surroundings. Mice are very agile and swift, and a frightened mouse might easily dart or leap away before you could catch it. Once on the floor, it might hide behind the furniture or slip away through a crack in the wall. Over the years, our children have lost a couple of mice that way. One of them used to come back and visit with the other mice in their cages, sniffing them through the wires, but she was always too quick for us to catch. Eventually we discovered that she was pregnant when she escaped, and we finally had to set traps for her and her growing family.

Some patience and a well-baited live trap can usually solve the problem of a runaway mouse. But it can be a difficult and trying experience. It is better to avoid the problem by taking extra care in handling new pet mice. Soon they will become so tame that you can let them scamper freely on your open hand, perch on your shoulder, or even take a nap in your pocket.

CHOOSING A MOUSE

Recently, while trying to find a couple of exotic varieties of mice, we called a pet shop that advertised "the biggest selection in New York City." "Sorry," we were told, "the only mice we have are the white ones." Although that pet shop did not live up to its ad, most of the shops in the small towns in our area feature a great variety of mice—mice with pure white fur and red eyes, glossy black mice, gray mice, tan mice, brown mice, spotted mice. The colored varieties of mice include both "selfs," whose fur is the same color all over the body, and "tan" varieties, with tan fur

*Mice come in many varieties.*

on their bellies regardless of the color of the rest of the fur. Some of the marked varieties have splotches of colored fur scattered over their bodies; others are very evenly marked with patches or bands of color—for example, the Dutch mice, whose markings resemble those of a Dutch rabbit. (That is a two-toned variety, with a broad belt of white fur around its middle and a blaze of white down its face.) Very hard to find (and, of course, more expensive) are unusual varieties like the Rex mice, with curly fur, and the angora mice, with long fur.

One curious variety is the waltzing mouse. Waltzers are bred not for color but for a type of behavior: they stagger and spin about in a sort of "dance" when they walk. These mice are not sick; because of their heredity, they are unable to develop a normal sense of balance.

*The angora mouse.*

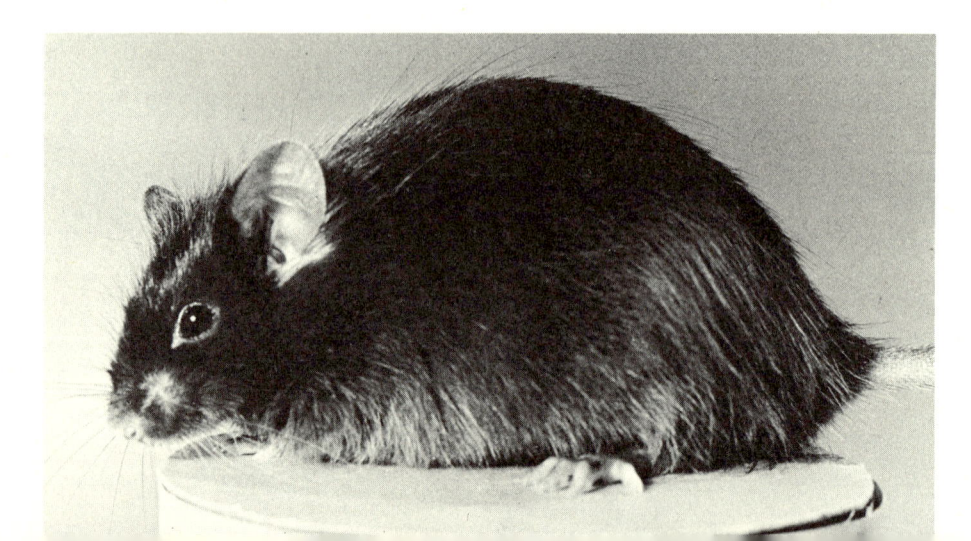

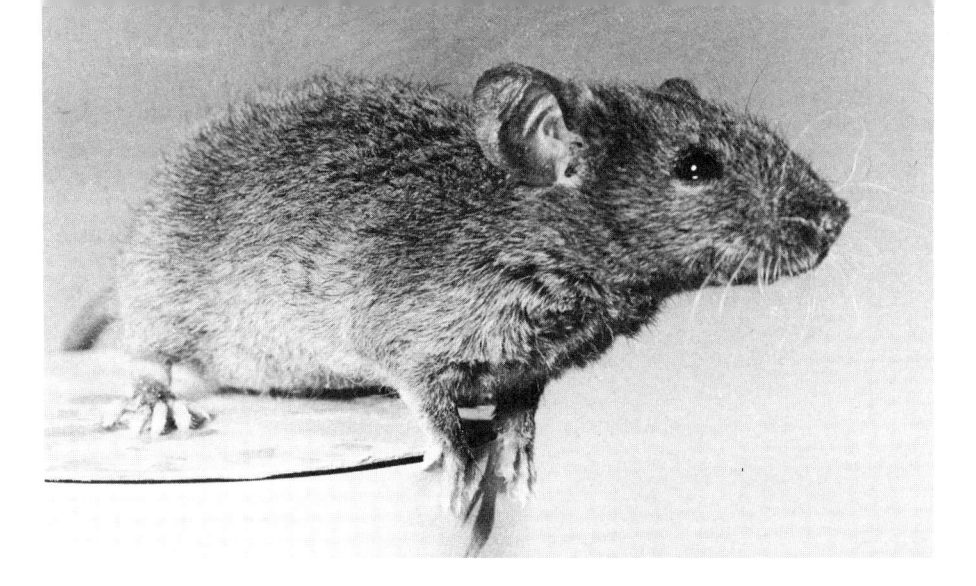

*The curly-haired Rex.*

The mouse you choose should be healthy looking, with bright eyes, alert ears, and sleek, glossy fur. Watch how it acts in the cage, and then out on the pet shop counter. You want a mouse that moves about actively and explores its surroundings, not one that sits hunched up in a corner, shivering.

How does the mouse act when it is being taken out of the cage? Does it struggle and bite, or does it rest confidently on the salesperson's hand? If the mouse acts wild, it has not been handled very much and is not yet used to people. A little wildness is not necessarily a reason for rejecting a mouse. With plenty of gentle handling, you can have it tame within a few days. But at least you will know beforehand what you will be facing and can avoid problems.

Many pet shops keep large numbers of mice together in a big common cage. In such cases, be especially careful to choose a mouse that looks healthy and alert, for overcrowding may contribute to illness among the mice. Another possible complication (which you may regard as either a problem or a bonus) is that mice living together in a big cage will probably have mated, if they are old enough. If you are interested in breeding mice, buying a female from such a cage can be a way to get a lot of mice for the price of one. But her litter may be a real surprise package if mice of different colors were kept together.

We have had two experiences with mice that were pregnant when we bought them. One, who had been raised in a very crowded cage, gave birth to a single large baby and then killed and ate it after a few days. (Eventually, after some time in our quieter home surroundings, she did bear and raise more normal litters.) Meecie, on the other hand, was a little tan-colored mouse who was sold to us as a "breeding female," guaranteed pregnant. About a week after we brought her home, she gave birth to a litter of ten healthy babies. She was a very good mother and raised her children conscientiously, even though she had been moved so recently to new surroundings. We were particularly surprised at her even-tempered patience, since we broke one of the standard animal-breeding rules and handled the babies regularly from the very first day of their lives—a practice that can make an animal mother so nervous and upset that she rejects her offspring. (Some of Meecie's young can be seen in the growth sequence pictures on pages 120–121.) But we wonder what the children's father looked like: some of the babies turned out to have tan fur like their mother's, some were a silvery gray, and some were white!

If you want to breed your mice—or if you *don't* want to breed your mice—an important thing to consider in choosing them is their sex. You can tell the sex of a mouse by looking at its underparts. The two body openings under the base of the tail are rather far apart in a male, and much closer together in a female. In a male, especially an adult,

*Sexing mice: the male is on the left, the female on the right.*

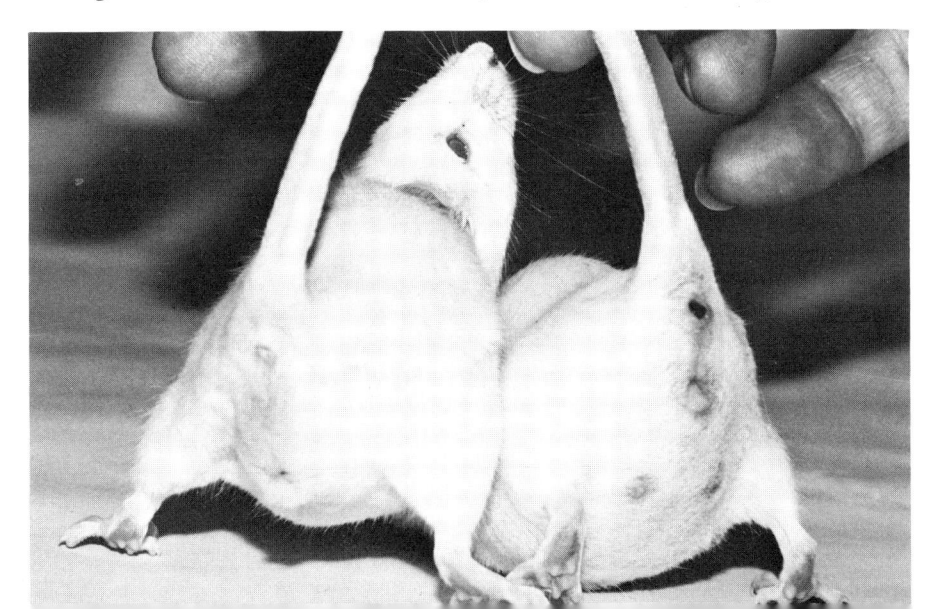

you can also see the scrotum hanging down like two seat cushions, one on each side. (The skin of the male mouse's "seat" may look somewhat darker than that on the rest of his body.) For breeding, you will need at least one male and one female, or perhaps a male and two females. If you want more than one mouse but don't want to cope with a population explosion, your best choice is to buy two or more females. Females do not produce the mousy odor, and they will live together peacefully in the same cage, while males together may fight.

## WHERE TO KEEP PET MICE

When we first started breeding mice, the only cages available were wire cages and aquariums. A wire cage can keep a mouse satisfactorily, especially if it has a removable tray on the bottom for cleaning. The mouse can enjoy some exercise by climbing on the wires. But it is not very much fun looking at your mice through the wire mesh or bars. An aquarium with clear glass sides, fitted with a wire mesh top, is much more satisfactory for mouse watching. (The mesh top will keep the mice from jumping or climbing out, and also protect them from cats and other animals.)

*Mouse cages: aquariums, plastic cages, wire cages.*

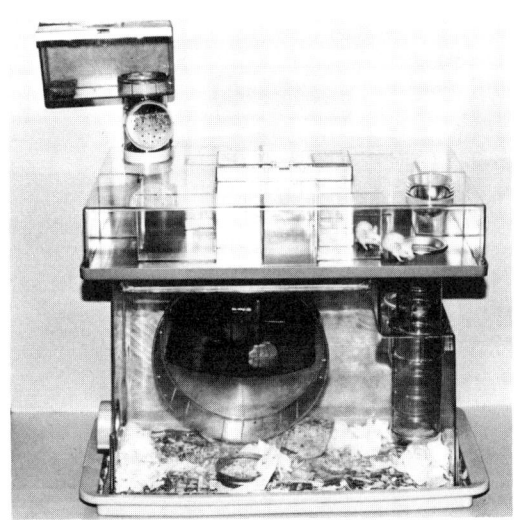

A wire cage can have another disadvantage. One wire cage that we own has bars about a centimeter (half an inch) apart. It works well enough for an adult mouse, but for young ones it is definitely not mouse-proof. We placed a litter of month-old mice, just separated from their mother, in the wire cage, and they seemed to melt right out through the bars. Each mouse's body looked at least twice as wide as the gap between the bars, but the mice easily stretched themselves out and squeezed through. Such a cage would also be a poor choice for a female raising a litter; the babies would continually fall out through the bars.

In recent years, a variety of plastic cages for gerbils and hamsters, such as those produced by Habitrail, have become available. We suspected that they would be suitable for mice, too, and we have found them generally satisfactory. The mice are held securely, and they are able to climb up the tubes to the "sky house" and work the various exercise wheels. We do have a few reservations, though. The Habitrail cages have a wire mesh floor over a removable tray. Adult mice do not seem to mind living on a wire mesh floor, but newborn mice are so tiny that they slip through the mesh into the tray of shavings underneath, and it is difficult for their mother to get them out again. The "deluxe" Habitrail cage, we have found, poses another problem. It has a

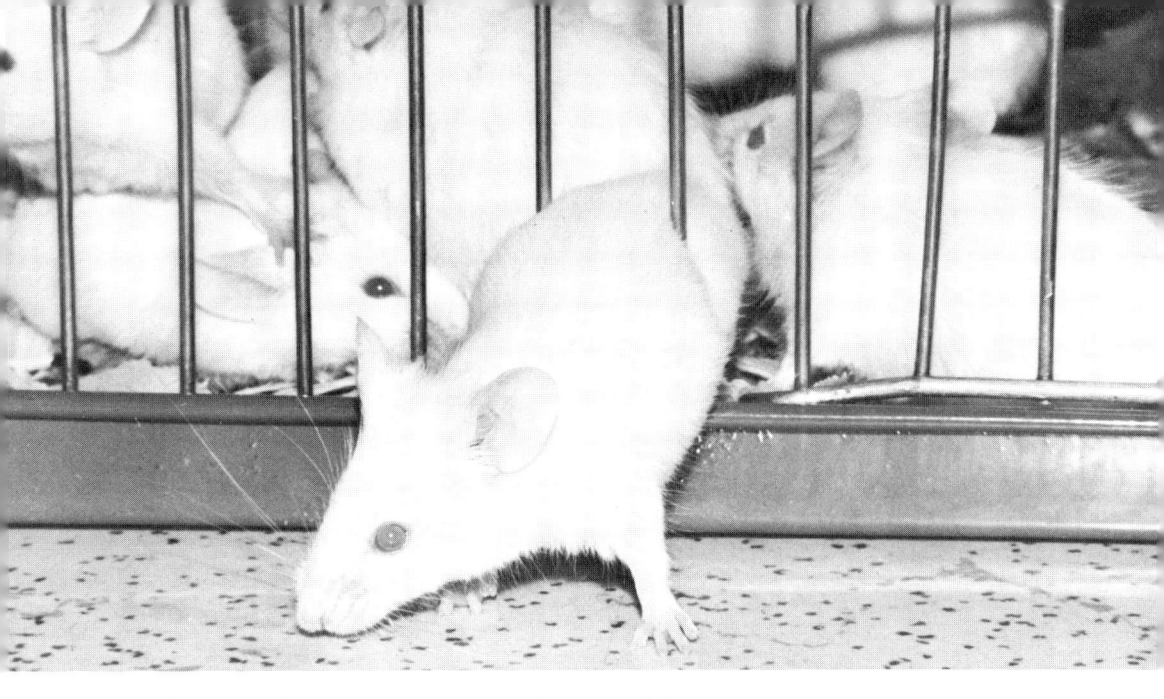

*The bars on this cage were spread too widely to keep young mice.*

large plastic exercise wheel, inside of which there is a little compartment that can be reached through a small hole. The mice love it. They sleep, rest, and take refuge in this cozy compartment. Unfortunately, it is rather difficult to get at them there—the whole exercise wheel must be taken apart. When it is that difficult to get to your mice, you will be less likely to take them out and play with them. Yet handling mice is the way to make them tame, and the less you handle them, the wilder and more likely to scamper away and hide inside the wheel they will become.

One mistake mouse raisers sometimes make is to get too small a cage. A mouse is a very small animal, but its ancestors were used to having the freedom of a whole house to roam in. It will be difficult for a pet mouse to stay happy and healthy in a little six-inch cage. Mouse breeders recommend a standard of about one square foot of floor space per mouse. A twelve- by twenty-inch aquarium would thus be about right for a pair of mice.

If you build a cage for mice, cover any wood parts with wire mesh. Pet mice are rodents, after all, and they might eventually chew their way out through bare wood. A wooden floor is also not a very good idea, because mouse urine will soak into it, and it will be almost impossible to keep clean.

Regardless of what kind of cage you choose, the mice will appreciate a little nest box and some soft material, such as paper tissues, to put inside it. They will shred the bedding material with their teeth and arrange it carefully in their sleeping area. An exercise wheel will help to keep them in condition. If the wheel squeaks, use a little vegetable oil to grease it, rather than machine oil, so that the mice will not become ill if they lick it. (We had five exercise wheels all merrily squeaking away in different keys before one of our sons thought of that trick.)

*The mice appreciate a nest box.*

*Running on an exercise wheel.*

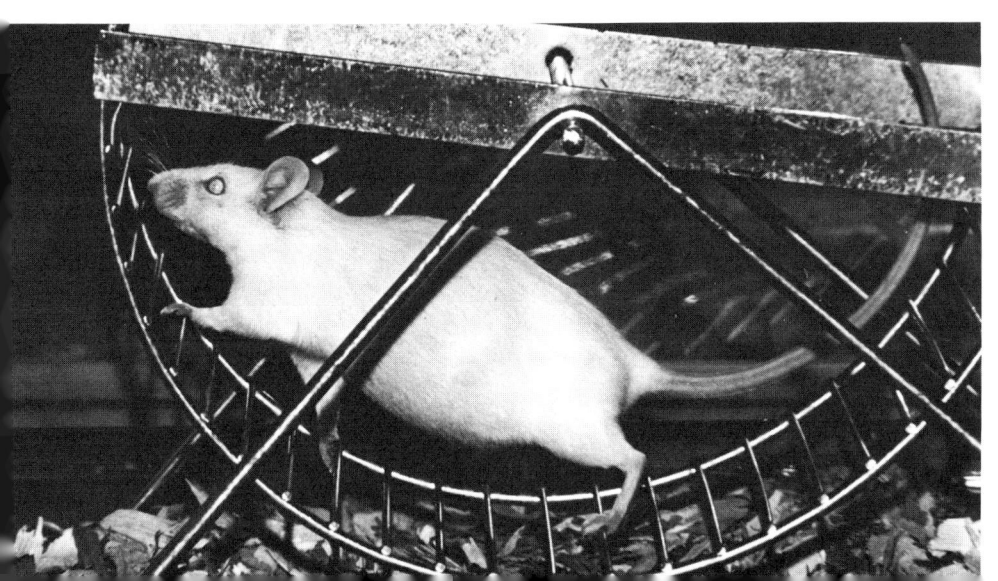

Food can be placed on the cage floor, or in a dish made of some material too hard to chew. A metal jar lid makes a convenient feeding dish for a mouse. An inverted bottle with a metal or glass tube extending from it is best for supplying water. The mice can drink the water as they need it, stretching up to take a drop at a time, and the water will stay clean. (If you try to give mice water in an open bowl, they will probably knock it over or drop bits of food and bedding in it, and babies might tumble into it and drown.) Make sure the tip of the tube from the water bottle

*The mouse holds a tidbit in its "hands" as it nibbles.*

is not in contact with bedding or other materials, which could act as a wick and drain the water out.

The bottom of the cage should be covered with clean wood shavings, sand, or some other absorbent material. Don't be tempted to use torn-up newspaper: the ink from the printing will make the mice dirty, and could even make them ill. Clean the cage out thoroughly at least once a week.

A friend of ours had a pet mouse that was allowed the run of the house. The cage door had broken, and she never bothered to fix it. The mouse came home to his cage to eat and sleep. The family cat left the mouse alone. But, unfortunately, one day someone let the barn cat in while the mouse was out of his cage—and that was the end of the mouse. So, for its own protection, even a very tame mouse should be caged securely unless you are there to supervise it.

## MICE AT PLAY

Mice are born acrobats. They love to leap from one place to another, and they cling not only with their feet, but also with their long, slender tails. You can make a fine trapeze for a mouse by hanging a pencil or popsicle stick from the roof of the cage with two thin wires. A round steak or chop bone on a string can serve as a combination trapeze and teething ring, to wear down those rodent teeth.

It is fun to watch a mouse on an exercise wheel. The mouse quickly gets the rhythm of the wheel, and keeps it turning as it runs. Now and then it may miss a step, or stop for a rest and let itself be carried around and around. Sometimes two mice will run on the wheel at the same time, keeping perfectly in step. They keep returning again and again to their play wheel. (Scientists in laboratories have attached counting devices to exercise wheels to see how much the mice actually run. One mouse ran the equivalent of ten miles in a night.)

An empty toilet paper roll makes an enjoyable addition to a mouse's cage. The mice run through the cardboard tunnel again and again, or hide inside and then pop out at one end.

Since the last time we raised mice, we have owned a variety of other rodents—guinea pigs, hamsters, and gerbils. After our experiences with those animals, which gnaw constantly on everything—keeping us awake with the twanging of their biting on the metal parts of their cages, reducing plastic nest boxes to rubble, shredding cardboard tubes or boxes to confetti in about five minutes flat—we were pleasantly surprised to become reacquainted with mice. Sometimes it seems as though our mice don't know they are rodents. No noise of biting on metal. (Plenty of noise from the exercise wheels, though—especially in the middle of the night.) No chunks bitten out around the doorways of plastic nest boxes. They haven't even chewed up their latest cardboard tunnel. But maybe they are just lazy rodents. Our son Robert informs us that our mice did reach out and chew holes in a sheet of paper and a plastic cover he had left next to a wire cage.


## WHAT TO FEED PET MICE

Some pet shops and feed-supply houses sell special foods for mice. They come as dry pellets or mixtures of seeds and grains that are easy to store and won't spoil. This kind of mouse food is the most convenient, and when a mouse is living on seeds and grains it will need little drinking water and will produce less urine. But special foods are not really needed. A mouse will eat almost anything you do. Mice can be fed on bits and scraps of the family's food. Whole-grain breads and cereals are very good for them. Bread soaked in a bit of milk makes a good supplement for a nursing mother and growing young mice. Mice also enjoy lettuce and other fresh greens, though such foods should be introduced in small amounts at first and stopped if the mice develop diarrhea. Carrot or apple peelings and an occasional bit of meat or hard-boiled egg are good foods for mice. So are nuts. We have also raised these rodents quite satisfactorily on dog biscuits!

Because a mouse is so small, it does not eat very much at a time. But it burns up energy very rapidly. (Its heart beats about six hundred and fifty times a minute, about ten times as fast as the human heart, and it also breathes much more rapidly than a human does.) So it needs to replace this energy by eating very often. Like its wild ancestors, which gathered seeds and grains in the fields, the pet mouse is a nibbler, eating small amounts of food all day long. It will not finish all the food you give it at one time, but will eat a little and then return to the food again and again. A supply of dry food should be left in the cage all the time. But if you feed your mouse fresh foods or table scraps, you must be careful to take away the leftovers before they spoil. If you go away for the weekend, be sure to leave an extra supply of food and water for pet mice, or arrange to have someone care for them. A pet mouse can starve to death if it goes without food for even one day.

## FUN WITH MICE

The more you handle a mouse, the tamer it will become. Soon it will enjoy being picked up and will look forward to play sessions outside its cage.

When you first start handling a mouse that is not yet used to people, it will be frightened. (Very young mice, not yet old enough to leave their mother, may jump when you try to pick them up, scattering in all directions like popcorn popping out of a pan.) It is a good idea to handle a new mouse only *inside* the cage for a few days, so it will not leap away and hurt itself.

If you frighten an untamed mouse, it may bite. The nips of a young mouse do not hurt, though they may startle you. But an adult mouse that has not yet been gentled by handling may sink its teeth painfully into your finger and hold on like a little bulldog, refusing to let go until you put it down. (One of us had to have a quick, unscheduled trip to the doctor for a tetanus booster the day Meecie came home from the pet shop; but up-to-date tetanus protection is a good thing to have anyway, even if you are not planning to handle mice.)

A mouse that has not yet been tamed should be picked up at first by the tail, an inch or two from the base. This

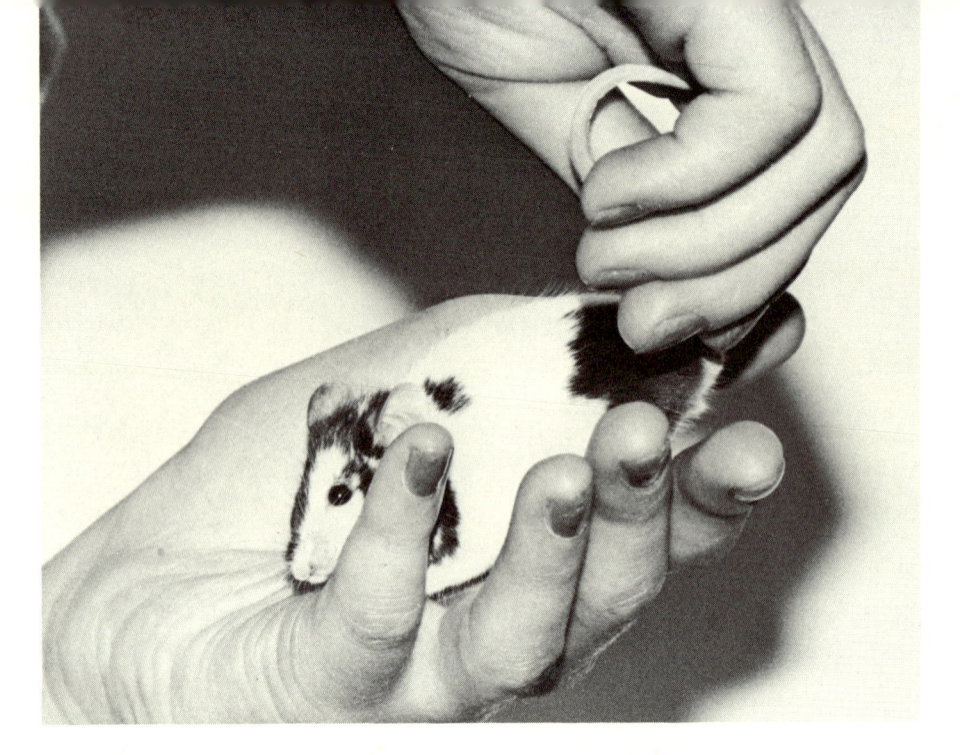

*In picking up a new mouse, it's wisest to hold it near the base of the tail.*

is not the best way to pick up mice generally, although it is the method used in laboratories; but with a mouse that may bite, it is the safest way. Lower the mouse promptly onto your open hand, so that it will have support for its feet and feel less insecure. A few tidbits of food waiting there may help to give it a positive feeling about the experience. After you have handled the mouse some, you will be able to scoop it into the palm of your hand, instead of picking it up by the tail.

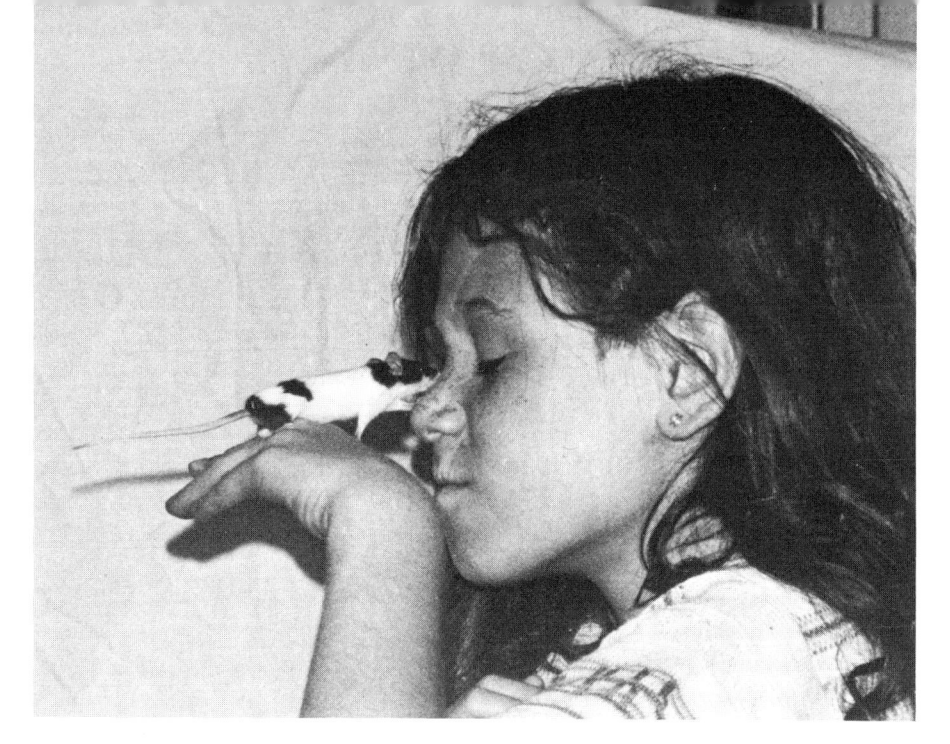

*When a mouse is tame, it will perch on your hand.*

When you are walking with a mouse, it is a good idea to cup your hand around it securely, so that it will not become frightened and leap away. (Don't squeeze! A mouse is delicate, and you are much stronger than it is.) Or hold its tail gently between your fingers while it rests on your hand, so you can stop it if it tries to jump.

With patience, you can teach a mouse to do some tricks, such as eating from your hand and climbing up your arm to perch on your shoulder. A mouse's natural curiosity makes it explore its surroundings. You can watch its movements, and when it does what you want, reward it with tidbits of a food it particularly likes, such as kernels of freshly cooked corn or small pieces of carrot. Take the training in easy stages and repeat it over a number of days, always rewarding the mouse.

*With gentle handling, soon the mouse will be tame and friendly.*

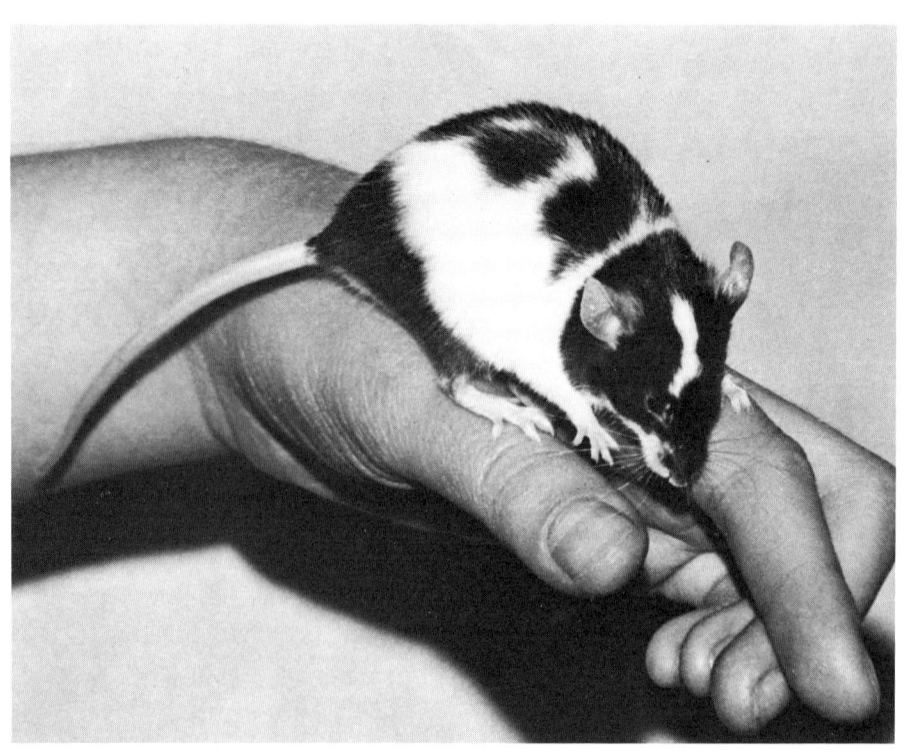

A pet mouse is just the right size to fit into toy cars and doll furniture. It will have fun exploring such toys, and will be amusing to watch and play with.

Mice are normally nocturnal animals, most active at dusk and into the wee hours of the night. (Many of the photographs in this book were taken about 2:00 A.M.) But that does not mean that they sleep solidly through the day and cannot be disturbed. A typical pet mouse will spend the daylight hours napping, waking to eat or run about, and then napping again. It will not mind being awakened to play during the day, as long as you do not wake it up too suddenly and give it a few minutes to gather its wits together before you pick it up.

*Just the right size for a dollhouse world.*

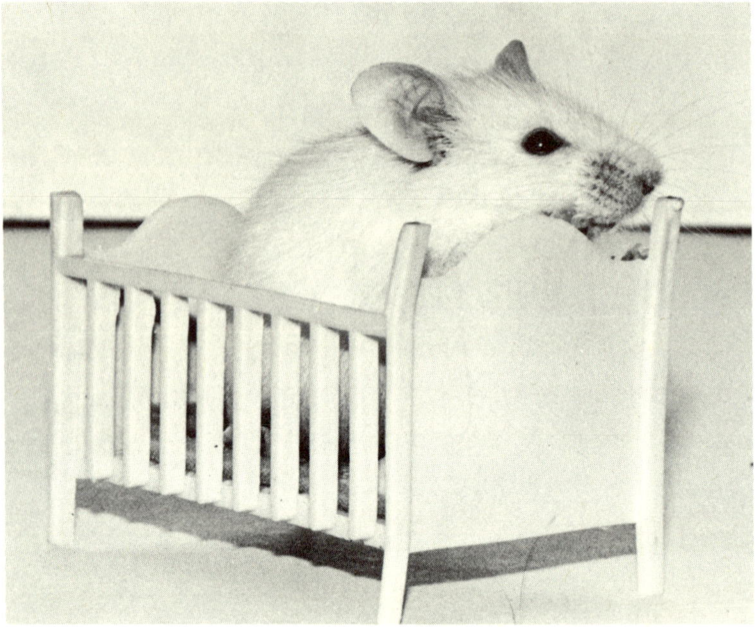

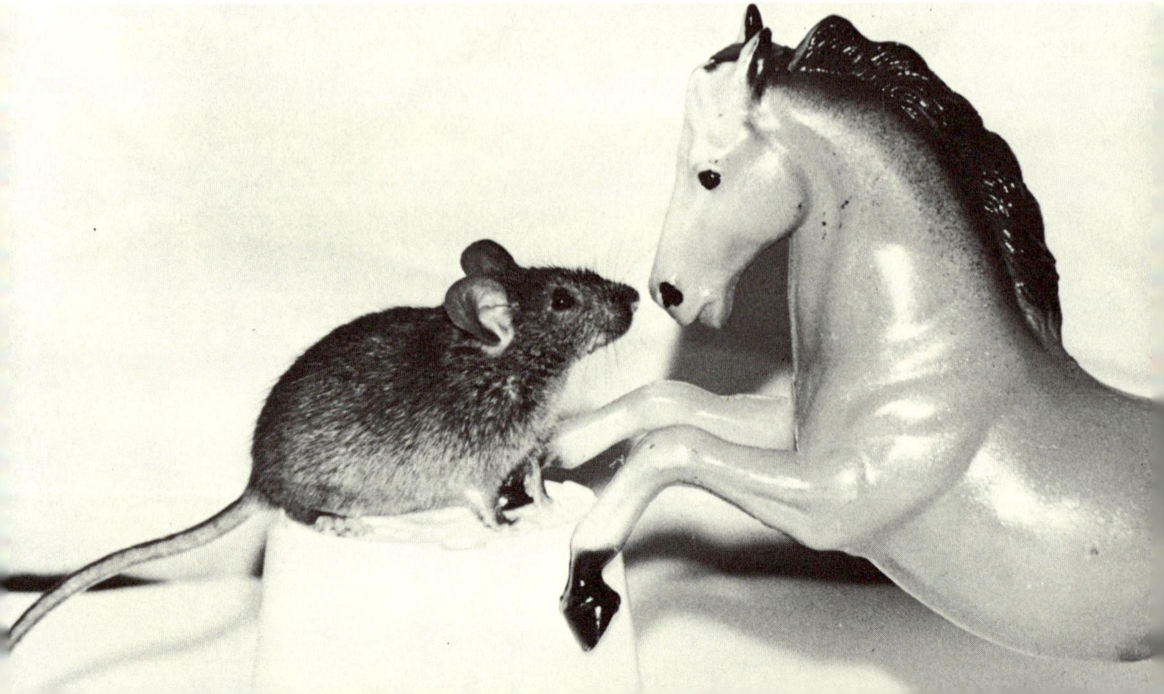

Our mice vary considerably in their daily activities. Meecie and her children seem to be awake and active for much of the day. Tony and Cleo sleep quite a bit during the day, but they alternate their naps with periods of eating, caring for their babies, and running on the exercise wheel. (All their mating has been during the day, after the litters were born the night before.) Celia, Tara, and Lucy, three females who share a cage, spend most of the daytime hours inside their little plastic house. We had originally given them two plastic houses, not knowing how three females in the same cage would get along, but they all moved into one house, stuffed full of bedding, and left the other empty. We eventually took the second house out and gave it to our black mouse Riki, who spends much of his day climbing up and down the wire bars of his cage and scampering upside down on the ceiling.

Mouse watching can provide hours of fascination. It is fun to see the mice scampering about, eating, and washing themselves like miniature house cats. A mouse carefully washes its face and hands after each meal, and it bends and twists to groom the rest of its body, keeping its fur clean and shining. Even the scaly tail gets regular baths with the mouse's washrag tongue.

It is interesting to offer mice a variety of foods and note

*Go, mouse, go!*

which ones they prefer. Some of our mice carefully pick out all the seeds in their dish and leave the mouse-food pellets, eating those only when they have no other choice. Most people think mice love cheese, but actually they usually prefer peanut butter.

 Wild mice kill and eat insects, and one evening we decided to see if pet mice would enjoy an insect treat. We placed a moth that had been fluttering around our porch light inside one of our mouse cages. The moth at first dropped to the floor of the cage and perched there motionless, trying to look like a wood shaving. The mice watched with interest when the moth first entered the cage, but then seemed to forget about it when it stopped moving. Then the moth flew up again. Its fluttering attracted Celia's attention, and as soon as it was within range she pounced, batted it to the floor of the cage, and promptly bit it. She ate the juicy center parts and left the wings.

RAISING MOUSE FAMILIES

It is fun to breed mice and watch them raise their litters. But before you decide to do so, consider this bit of arithmetic. Suppose that a pair of mice have a litter of ten, five males and five females. Now you have twelve mice. In just three weeks, the original parents can have another litter of ten (that makes twenty-two mice), in three weeks more another litter of ten (thirty-two mice), and in another three weeks still another litter (forty-two mice). By that time, the first litter is old enough to breed, and each pair can have its own litter. With another litter from their parents by that time, you have a hundred and two mice, just twelve weeks after the first litter was born. Now the second litter is ready to breed; three weeks later you have two hundred twelve mice, and the third litter is ready to breed, too. (By this time we are getting tired of arithmetic, but if you are not, you can figure out how many mice you will have at the end of a year.)

All these numbers, of course, represent what would happen under ideal conditions. Your mice might have litters smaller than ten (though the litters could also be larger); they might not breed again right away; and you can control the process by separating the young mice according to sex so that they cannot breed at all. But even if you allow just one pair to breed, you could quickly find yourself in the mouse-raising business, and you need to have some idea of what you are going to do with all the babies. (We have been lucky enough to find a pet shop that, so far, has been willing to buy as many mice as we can supply.)

The first time we raised mice, we followed the standard laboratory procedure of keeping them all separate and allowing a male to visit each female in turn. That is a good way to keep your records straight and know just what kind of babies to expect and when to expect them. But since then we have raised hamsters, which fight viciously if you try to keep them in a cage together, and gerbils, which live happily in mated pairs, both parents helping to raise and care for the young. We were curious to see what would happen if we left a pair of mice together after mating.

The experiment was a brilliant success. Antony and Cleopatra settled down happily in their snug little nest box (we had splurged and bought them the deluxe two-story plastic house) inside a roomy aquarium. They seemed a devoted couple, eating, sleeping, and running on their exercise wheel together. Cleo began to bulge out on the sides and exercised even harder. Then one night, tiny squeakings from the nest box announced the arrival of the first litter. The next morning, Tony was sleeping outside while Cleo was in the house with the babies. Aha, we thought, she kicked him out! At that point, Cleo emerged from her house, and after a brief run around the cage, she and Tony mated. So much for that theory.

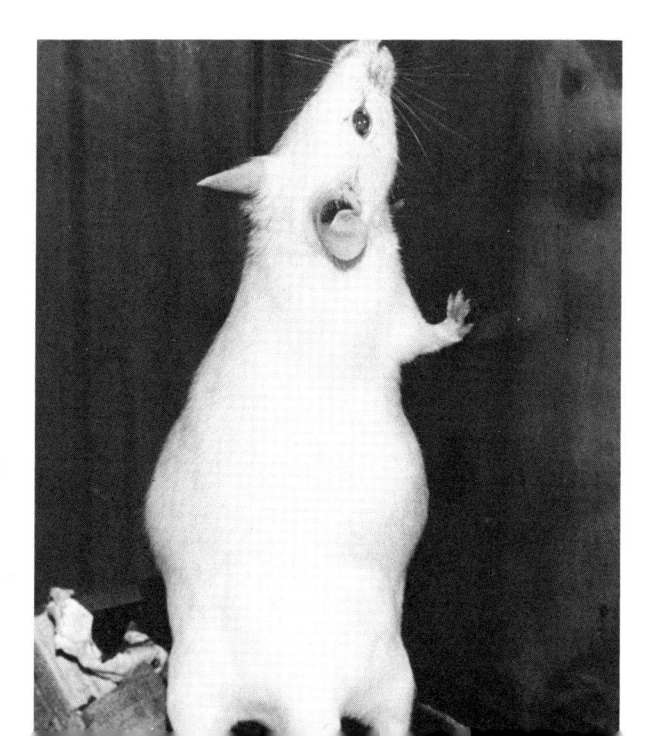

*Cleo began to bulge on the sides . . .*

As the days passed, we observed them. Sometimes Tony was outside the nest and Cleo was inside with the babies. Sometimes Cleo was outside and Tony was babysitting in the nest. Sometimes they were all in there together. Sometimes Cleo brought some or all of the babies out. Meanwhile, according to their own mouse logic, Cleo and Tony played the rearrange-the-bedding game. Sometimes they stuffed the little house so full of shredded tissue that we couldn't see anything through the windows at all. At other times they pulled out every shred and left the nest bare. Probably they were trying to adjust the temperature and humidity in the nest.

Because we were trying to determine whether a mated pair of mice could successfully raise their litter together, we left Tony and Cleo strictly alone except for feeding them and cleaning their cage occasionally. We caught glimpses of Cleo feeding her young and both parents moving and grooming the babies. But for two weeks we didn't try to handle the babies, or even count them.

Meanwhile, we had another litter of mice to observe at close range: Meecie had her litter of ten on the same night Cleo gave birth. How strange the babies looked at first— not like rodents at all. They had no hair, and their pink bodies looked like plump little worms. Their skin was so

*Cleo, feeding her litter.*

thin and delicate that each one's milk-filled stomach showed through as a tiny white crescent on its belly. The eyes of the newborn mice were sealed shut, and they did not yet have the pointed noses of their parents—they had flat little puppy dog faces. They were completely helpless. They could not walk or care for themselves. All they could do was wriggle about and drink their mother's milk.

Meecie took her motherhood seriously. She made a soft nest for her babies out of shredded tissue, and each time we opened the cage, she fluffed the bedding up over the babies, as if to try to hide them. When we had the problem of wriggly babies slipping through the wire mesh floor of the cage, we fixed up a cardboard floor for the compartment in which Meecie had made her nest. We carefully replaced all the bedding after we had inserted the floor. Apparently all our bustling about that day, and on the next day when we took out one of the tiny mice for photographing, upset the mother mouse, for she moved her bedding and all her children into the other compartment of her cage. Worried about the wire floor, we moved everything back. Within half an hour, carrying her babies one by one in her mouth, Meecie again had things the way *she* wanted them. Although we continued to take one or more of the young mice out each day, and Meecie watched us warily and grabbed her babies back as soon as we were finished with them, she did not try to move the nest again.

Both Meecie and Cleo generally left all their babies in one big pile, and there was a great scrambling and squeaking at feeding time. We once had a mouse, though, who divided her litter of thirteen into two separate piles of five and eight, at opposite ends of the cage. Afraid that she might overlook some of them, we moved the babies all back together. The mother mouse promptly divided them into the two piles again and visited each pile in turn. We are not sure how she figured out the arithmetic, but her method worked very well: since a mouse has only eight teats, all the babies in each pile could feed at once, without having to wait for a brother or sister to finish.

The little mice grew quickly. By about ten days, each had a full coat of fine, soft fur, and at fourteen days they began to open their eyes. Even before their eyes were open they were moving about actively, roaming all over the cage. They began to nibble on solid food, and by the time they were three weeks old, they were getting old enough to survive without their mother.

We have read that if a mouse is nursing a litter, especially a large one, the development of the next litter may be delayed by as much as several days. Cleo is apparently a more heroic

*See how quickly the little mice grow.*

13 DAYS

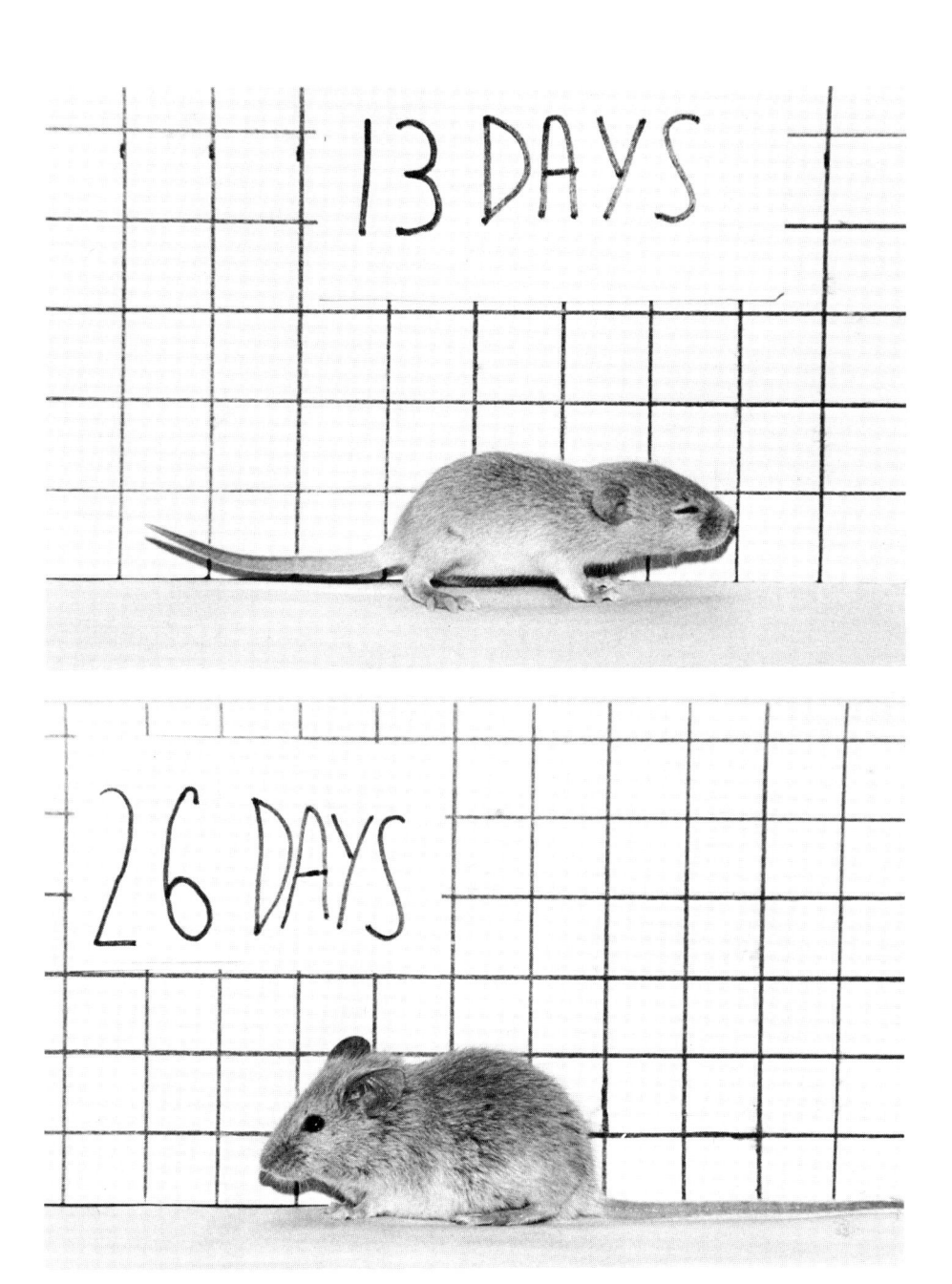

26 DAYS

type. Just twenty days after the birth of her first litter of ten, tiny squeakings were again to be heard from the nest box. We left the older litter with her for a couple of days while we got another cage, and there did not seem to be any problems. But we were not sure how long Cleo's good humor would last with two sets of babies around her, so we took the three-week-old mice out.

Cleo's new litter totaled eighteen, and she mated again right after they were born. The large litter kept Cleo busy constantly, feeding and cleaning, and we often noticed Tony babysitting. Two of the babies never seemed to get their fair share of Cleo's milk—by the time it was their turn, she would be out of patience and push them aside. These two were "runts," and they grew and developed more slowly than their littermates. They were not only smaller, but their fur came in later and they opened their eyes later than the others. If we had had another nursing mother mouse available, one who was not so overloaded, we might have tried to get her to "adopt" a few of Cleo's babies.

To get a mother mouse to accept babies that are not her own, you can wipe them with some of the bedding from her nest so they will smell right to her. Or you can try putting a bit of Vaseline on her nose so she cannot smell them at first; by the time her sense of smell has recovered, they will smell just like her own children.

When Cleo's second litter was exactly twenty days old, she gave birth to another litter of fourteen. What a mouse!

Theoretically, any litter of baby mice should contain about half males and half females. But in any particular litter, the results can be quite different. Cleo's first litter, for example, included seven males and only three females, while Meecie's litter, born at the same time, had six females and four males. In Cleo's second litter there were nine of each sex.

Well cared for and protected, pet mice may live for three years or more.

# MICE IN THE LABORATORY

The foods you ate today probably contained substances that were tested on mice. The last time you were sick and took medicine prescribed by your doctor, the drug you received almost certainly was developed and tested with the help of mice. Manufacturers of shampoos, hair dyes, lipsticks, and various other cosmetics test their products for safety on mice before they place them on sale. Mice are probably the most commonly used laboratory animals—close to thirty million mice are raised for laboratory use each year in the United States alone. These tiny rodents are helping us to learn more about ourselves, and have already helped to save many millions of human lives.

Mice make especially good laboratory animals. They are small and easy to care for. They eat most of the same foods people do, and catch many of the same diseases. They breed so quickly that scientists can easily have large numbers to work with, and can follow effects through many generations.

Typical laboratory mice are quite different from ordinary house mice. They have been specially bred over thousands of generations. They are much tamer and gentler than their wild cousins, and they also breed faster.

Today there are many laboratory strains of mice with pedigrees that are exactly known over many more generations than those of any human. Some of these strains have been specially bred to develop certain conditions or diseases, such as overweight, tooth decay, or cancer.

Within each special line of laboratory mice, scientists have used a technique called inbreeding. They have mated parents and children, brothers and sisters, so that down through the generations the offspring become more and more alike.

*Each of these mice represents a different inbred strain, used in scientific research.*

It is possible to order a shipment of a particular line of mice and know that the animals will be just like mice of the same line that have been raised halfway across the world. In fact, even grade school students can obtain specially inbred mice for classroom projects and experiments.

Scientists consider it extremely important to use inbred animals in research. Good research must be reproducible: any scientist in any laboratory anywhere in the world should be able to repeat the experiments and get the same results; otherwise no one could be sure the results were really correct. Unrelated mice are just as different from one another as unrelated people. They may react quite differently to the same drugs, foods, or conditions of life. Mice in the same family, much like people in the same family, are more alike than unrelated mice. And highly inbred mice are so much alike that they are nearly "identical twins." Their reactions to drugs and various other influences are also very much alike. (In fact, scientists can even transplant skin successfully from one mouse to another of the same highly inbred line. In unrelated animals, such a patch of transplanted skin would be rejected by the body and soon die off.) Scientists testing a drug or other product on inbred mice are therefore much more likely to get repeatable results than if they used unrelated animals.

## UNDERSTANDING DISEASE

Mice have played an important role in unraveling the mysteries of human disease. Experiments on these animals have helped in the development of treatments and cures for pneumonia, tuberculosis, diphtheria, typhoid fever, kidney diseases, and many other ailments.

A scientist who is trying to find a cure for a particular disease can inject the germs that cause that disease into a number of healthy mice. When they become sick, the researcher can give some of them a new drug to see whether it helps the animals to get better. It is very important to have what the scientist calls "controls"—animals that are not given any of the drug at all. The experimenter carefully watches the animals that were given the experimental drug and the control animals, comparing the results in the two groups: how many animals die, how many get well, and how quickly they get well. This helps the researcher find out how effective the new drug really is. If *all* the animals received the drug and then got well, the experimenter would not know whether it was the drug that helped them. Perhaps they would have gotten better without any treatment at all.

In experiments using mice, rats, and other laboratory animals, the new "miracle drugs" have been tested before they have been used on humans. Researchers have not only been able to discover what drugs are helpful, but also have learned how much of a particular drug should be used to get the desired effect without harming the patient. (Too little of a drug might not cure the disease, while too much could make the patient ill. This is particularly true of cancer drugs, with which doctors try to kill cancer cells without killing too many normal body cells.) Vaccines that protect people against diseases such as diphtheria, polio, and influenza have also been developed using laboratory mice. Even after they are developed, new batches of vaccines and drugs are routinely tested on mice to make sure they are safe and effective before they are released for use on people.

One of the most terrible diseases in the world today is cancer. Special lines of inbred mice have been raised to help in the fight against this dread disease. Some of these special breeds almost always come down with cancer at some time in their lives. In fact, it is often possible to predict that a particular mouse will develop a particular kind of cancer, such as breast cancer or leukemia, and even to know ahead of time just about how old the mouse will be when the cancer appears. When researchers know that certain mice are going to develop cancer, they can try various drugs and other treatments to see if they can keep cancer from starting, or cure it after it appears. Thousands of chemicals have been tested for anticancer activity on mice, and hundreds of promising approaches are being tried. Injections of a substance chemically related to vitamin A seem to help prevent cancer. Scientists have used tiny magnets to move an iron-containing substance through an animal's bloodstream until it blocks off the blood supply that feeds a cancerous tumor. Other researchers have had mice with cancer breathe a mixture of hydrogen and oxygen, and their tumors have shriveled up and dropped off.

Researchers using mice are exploring the causes of cancer and how normal cells can suddenly go out of control. They treat the mice with X rays and other kinds of radiation, as well as with various chemicals. They are especially interested in the effects of chemicals that people come in contact with in their daily lives, such as the substances in some types of insulation, and the artificial sweetener saccharin, which is used in diet drinks and many foods.

Some cancer researchers believe that viruses play a role in causing cancer. They hope to isolate such viruses and then make vaccines to protect people against them. Experiments with mice have produced some interesting results. For example, there is a strain of mice that usually develops breast cancer. At first researchers thought that this was an example of a hereditary disease, passed on from parents to children. But then they found that mice of this inbred strain do not usually develop cancer if they are taken from their mothers right after birth and raised by foster mothers of a different strain. On the other hand, mice of a strain that *does not* normally develop breast cancer do come down with this disease rather often if they are nursed by foster mothers of the cancer strain. Apparently something in the mothers' milk is transmitting the cancer, and researchers believe it is a virus. Scientists are also experimenting to see if viruses are involved in other types of cancer—for example, leukemia.

Some of the mice being used in disease research spend all their lives in special stainless steel or plastic film isolators. Researchers handle them and care for them with special airtight gloves sealed into the isolator, or with remote-controlled mechanical devices. These mice are completely germ-free unless a researcher purposely introduces one particular kind of bacterium or virus to study its effects. Such animals make good controls in disease experiments, because they are not carrying other germs that might confuse the results. In one series of studies with germfree animals, researchers found that tooth decay will not occur, even on a diet full of sugar, unless certain kinds of bacteria are present in the mouth.

*The mouse in this plastic film isolator lives in a completely germfree world.*

## TOWARD BETTER DIETS

Scientists have learned a great deal about the foods we eat and how they affect our health through experiments with laboratory mice. Like people, these rodents can eat almost anything. They need very much the same sort of proteins, vitamins, and other nutrients that we do. (One difference is that mice can make their own supplies of vitamin C, while we must obtain this substance from foods. Some researchers, studying the amounts of vitamin C that mice produce in their bodies under various conditions, have suggested that we humans probably need larger amounts of this vitamin for good health than nutritionists previously believed.)

Scientists make up special diets and feed them to laboratory mice. They can leave out some important nutrient and watch what happens to the animals. Often the effects are very similar to the symptoms of some human diseases that are caused by bad diet, and researchers working with laboratory animals can find out how best to cure and prevent the human diseases.

Laboratory mice are also used to test new food additives—substances that are added to foods to give them color or flavor, or to keep them from spoiling. Only after these sub-

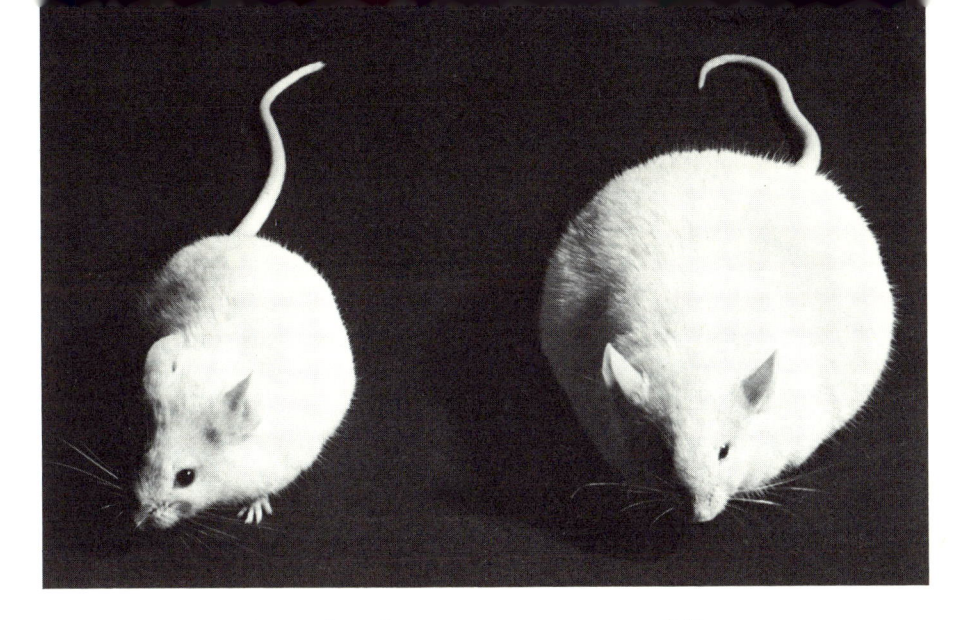

*The mouse on the right, shown next to a normal littermate, grew obese after a single dose of gold thioglucose.*

stances prove to be safe for laboratory animals are they tested for use in human food.

Sometimes the results of diet experiments are surprising. Researchers testing the additive BHT, which is put in cereals and other foods to keep them from spoiling when they are exposed to the air, discovered not only that it is safe, but that mice receiving it actually live *longer* than mice on a diet without BHT. Similar results were obtained in tests of vitamin E, which has the same kind of chemical effect as BHT. (Both are antioxidants, which protect foods from being oxidized, or chemically changed by the oxygen in the air.)

## RESEARCH ON AGING

Mice are almost ideal animals for experiments on aging. They are enough like humans that the results of studies on them might be applicable to us, too. Yet with a normal mouse life span of only a few years, researchers can test their theories about aging and results before they themselves are old and gray.

Researchers have found that various changes in diet can lengthen the lives of mice. Feeding mice a limited diet, low in protein, from the time of weaning on seems to slow down the development of mice and make them live longer. But researchers are wary about trying to use diets like that for people, for fear of stunting their mental and physical development. Experiments with antioxidants such as BHT and vitamin E are more promising. Other researchers have extended the lives of mice by feeding them a diet low in unsaturated fats, or by giving them a substance found in chick-peas.

Another group of researchers transplanted thymus glands from young mice into older ones. Some of the mice who received the transplants lived about one-third longer than normal. And they survived that long even though a deadly virus epidemic swept through the laboratory during the experiment, killing many of the mice in the colony. Getting a thymus transplant might not be a very practical way to lengthen your life, but researchers are studying some recently discovered hormones produced by the thymus gland. If these chemicals can be produced in large quantities, injections of them might be used to lengthen human lives.

## MINIATURE ASTRONAUTS

In space research, mice have many advantages as "miniature astronauts." Because they are much smaller than people and most other animals, they can fit comfortably into small satellites and spacecraft. Yet they are much more like us than insects or molds or other small living things that have been used in space research. Results obtained in experiments on mice are much more likely to be similar to the results that would be obtained with humans. Mice also breed so quickly that within months scientists can find out what effects weightlessness and other conditions of space travel will have on future generations.

Before the first human astronauts went out into space, mice were raised for many generations in machines that simulated weightless conditions. They were also raised in giant centrifuges that created a stronger gravity than Earth's—the kind of gravity astronauts would experience on one of the larger planets, or in a spacecraft during acceleration. The researchers had expected that life under a higher gravity than we have on Earth would be hard on the animals, and that they might become sickly. Surprisingly, that did not happen. Mice raised for many generations in a centrifuge at two and a half "G's" not only stayed healthy and bred normally, but actually lived longer than mice usually do on Earth.

Later, mice were sent up in specially designed cages inside rockets and satellites, and circled the globe as astronauts.

## STUDIES OF HEREDITY

One of the most fascinating areas of research with mice is the study of heredity. It is common knowledge that children usually look like their parents. But they don't always— and even when they do, they may be different from the parents in other respects. (This is true of nearly every living thing.) The study of how traits—such as the color of eyes or hair, the shape of the face or body, the kind of teeth or nails or claws—are passed on from parents to their offspring is called genetics. People who study heredity are referred to as geneticists.

Geneticists can study the inheritance of many different traits in mice, and their work helps us to understand the inheritance of similar traits in humans. The sleek fur of mice, for example, just like the hair of human beings, comes in many different colors. There are albino mice, which have white fur and red eyes because their bodies are unable to make the dark pigment called melanin. There are also black mice, brown mice, cinnamon-colored mice, and mice of many other colors. Some mice are all the same color, while others are spotted. Just as people may have curly or straight hair, there are curly- and straight-haired mice. Scientists have found that many diseases run in mouse families, just as some diseases run in human families.

You might wonder why geneticists bother to study heredity in animals when it would seem that heredity in human beings is more important and interesting. Scientists have found that heredity is basically the same in all animals, so that learning about how the color of fur or eyes or a tendency to come down with a particular disease is inherited in mice can provide insights into how people inherit similar traits.

It is much easier to experiment with mice than with people. For one thing, you cannot ask a man and woman to marry and have children simply because you think it would make an interesting experiment. When people do marry, they usually do not have very many children. However, geneticists can learn the most when they have large numbers of offspring to work with. Since mice often have a dozen or more young at a time and geneticists can mate any pair they want to, mice are much better to work with than people.

Another problem in studying heredity in humans is that it takes such a long time for a baby to grow up and have children of its own. Most people do not have children until they are twenty years old or older. Mice can begin having young when they are only a few months old. A geneticist can study a number of generations in a single year.

From their studies of heredity in mice, scientists have learned a great deal about how various diseases and conditions are inherited. They have applied their knowledge of mouse heredity to the breeding of special strains of mice that can be used as "models" of human ailments—for example, a strain of mice whose teeth decay easily, and another mouse strain whose members tend to get fat. The Jackson Laboratory in Bar Harbor, Maine, is a leader in mouse breeding and research, and has produced many special mouse strains that are used by researchers all over the world.

Mice of one of the Jackson Laboratory strains carry a hereditary form of diabetes that is very similar to the disease that occurs in humans. Mice of this strain were the first animals in which diabetes could be studied, and they provide a convenient model for testing new treatments for the disease. But breeding diabetic mice presents some special problems, because animals with the disease have difficulty producing young. The Jackson Laboratory breeders use two methods to get around the difficulty. They can breed diabetic mice from parents who are carrying the trait but do not develop the disease themselves. Or they can transplant the ovaries of a diabetic mouse into a normal mouse. The normal mouse then mates and raises litters of young that are genetically the children of the diabetic mouse that supplied the ovaries.

Another unusual and valuable mouse strain bred at the Jackson Laboratory and shipped to researchers all around the world is the hairless mouse. The bare skin of this mouse is ideal for testing drugs that are made in the form of oint-

*The hairless mouse has been especially valuable in cancer research.*

ments or creams, and also for testing cosmetics. Hairless mice also have a greater-than-usual tendency to develop leukemia, and they are being used in the study of this form of cancer.

The Jackson Laboratory also breeds mice that develop muscular dystrophy. These animals have proved very useful in the study of this dreadful disease, which strikes mostly children and teenagers.

Cell biologists have recently been conducting some very unusual experiments on mice. With microsurgery, they can take the hereditary information out of a tiny single cell and insert different hereditary information from another. One group of researchers has announced the cloning of a mouse: the growth of a normal mouse from a tiny single-celled egg whose own nucleus, containing the hereditary material, was destroyed and replaced by the nucleus of a cell from a mouse embryo of a different strain. The "cloned" mouse looked just like the parents of the embryo that supplied the nucleus, and not like the mother that gave birth to it.

Another group of researchers is doing something even stranger. By mixing cells from two different embryos and then putting the cells back inside the body of a mother mouse, they are growing mice that have four parents instead of two. Scientists refer to these unusual mice as chimeras. If one of the embryos came from an albino mouse line and the other from a black strain, the chimera that is born from the mixture is a "mosaic" mouse, with patches of black and white fur showing which parts of its body developed from which cells. Researchers are using chimera mice in the study of cancer and other diseases.

## STUDIES OF LEARNING AND BEHAVIOR

Mice are also being used in a variety of other laboratory studies. These rodents can be trained to find their way through mazes, learning and remembering the correct turns to receive a reward of food at the end of the maze. They can also learn to press a lever to get a reward. Such studies

*The spotted chimera mouse was born from a combination of embryos from an albino mouse and another inbred strain.*

have various applications. Drug researchers, for example, routinely test the effects of new drugs on memory and learning. If a particular drug makes a mouse learn a maze more quickly or slowly, or makes it forget what it has learned, the drug might have similar effects on people.

In an interesting series of experiments at Jackson Laboratory, researchers trained mice to get a portion of sweetened wheat cereal by poking one paw into a feeding tube in a glass-walled observation box. They found that about half the mice are naturally right-handed, and half are naturally left-handed—in contrast to humans, the majority of whom are right-handed. Once a mouse had learned the feeding routine, the researchers switched it to a box with the feeding tube fastened either at the far left side of the front wall or at the far right, rather than conveniently in the middle. In these "biased worlds," it was easy enough for the mouse to reach into the tube with one paw, but very awkward with the other. About 90 percent of the mice adapted easily to the new setup, taking out their food reward with whichever paw the box favored. But about 10 percent of the mice could not adapt, remaining stubbornly right-handed or left-handed even when using their preferred paw was very difficult and awkward.

Studies of learning in mice and other small laboratory animals are bringing us important insights into the processes of memory and learning, which may have applications for humans. Tiny electrodes inserted into the animals' brains can be used to stimulate various kinds of behavior or to transmit and record "brain waves" that indicate what parts of the brain—even individual nerve cells!—are working. Delicate brain surgery has revealed further information on the learning process. Researchers have even isolated chemicals from animals' brains that seem to act as "memory molecules," transmitting specific learned experiences. The first of these chemicals to be discovered was isolated from the brains of animals trained to fear the dark. When this chemical, scotophobin, is injected into the brain of an untrained mouse, that mouse, too, avoids dark places. The study of scotophobin and the other "memory molecules" may someday lead to effective treatments for people who suffer from memory losses.

Commensal mice may raid our pantries and even spread disease. Plagues of wild mice may destroy crops. But with all the knowledge that laboratory mice have provided, they have more than paid for any damage done by their relatives.

# HOW THE RODENTS ARE RELATED

## SUBORDER SCIUROMORPHA (squirrel-like)
Seven families, including:
Squirrels, prairie dogs, gophers,
chipmunks, beavers, woodchucks

Heteromyidae (pocket mice)
- *Dipodomys* (kangaroo rat)
- *Perognathus* (pocket mouse)
- *Microdipodops* (kangaroo mouse)

## SUBORDER HYSTRICOMORPHA (porcupinelike)
Sixteen families, including:
Porcupines, cavies (guinea pigs and
their relatives), chinchillas

## SUBORDER MYOMORPHA (mouselike)
Ten families, including:
Cricetidae (ancient mice, "the squeaking ones")
- SUBFAMILY CRICETINAE (hamsters and New World mice and rats)
  - *Cricetus, Cricetulus, Mesocricetus* (hamsters)
  - *Neotoma* (wood rat)
  - *Onychomys* (grasshopper mouse)
  - *Oryzomys* (rice rat)
  - *Peromyscus* (white-footed mouse)
  - *Phenacomys* (tree mouse)
  - *Pitymys* (pine mouse)
  - *Reithrodontomys* (American harvest mouse)
  - *Sigmodon* (cotton rat)

SUBFAMILY MICROTINAE (lemmings and voles)
  *Clethrionomys* (red-backed mouse)
  *Dicrostonyx* (snow lemming)
  *Lemmus* (Norway lemming)
  *Microtus* (meadow and field mice)
  *Ondatra* (muskrat)

SUBFAMILY GERBILLINAE (gerbils)
  *Gerbillus* (sand rats)
  *Meriones* (Mongolian gerbil)

Muridae (modern mice, "the mousy ones")
  SUBFAMILY MURINAE (Old World mice and rats)
    *Acomys* (spiny mouse)
    *Apodemus* (yellow-necked mouse and long-tailed field and wood mice of Europe)
    *Micromys* (European harvest mouse)
    *Mus musculus* (house mouse)
    *Rattus norvegicus* (brown rat)
    *Rattus rattus* (black rat)
    Gliridae (dormice)
      *Glis* (common dormouse)
      *Muscardinus* (hazel mouse)

  Zapodidae (jumping mice)
    *Napaeozapus*
    *Zapus*

  Dipodidae (jerboas)
    *Jaculus*

# FOR FURTHER READING

Cahalane, Victor H. *Mammals of North America*. New York: Macmillan Co., 1966.

Hirschhorn, Howard. *All About Mice*. Neptune City, N.J.: T.F.H. Publications, 1974.

Lauber, Patricia. *Of Man and Mouse*. New York: Viking Press, 1971.

Le Roi, David. *Fancy Mice, Rats and Gerbils*. London: Kaye and Ward, 1976.

McLoughlin, John C. *The Animals Among Us*. New York: Viking Press, 1978.

Roberts, Mervin F. *Mice as Pets*. Neptune City, N.J.: T.F.H. Publications, 1977.

Smith, K. W. *Mice and Rats*. London: Bartholomew, 1976.

# INDEX

Page numbers in *italics* refer to photographs

*Acomys: see* spiny mouse
adaptability, 35–37, 46–47
Aesop's fables, 21–22
aging research, 134–35
Alice in Wonderland, 26, *26,* 61
ancestors of house mouse, 3
angora mouse, 90, *90*
antioxidants, 133–34
*Apodemus: see* yellow-necked mouse
Apollo Smintheus, 28
Aricharpax, 32
astronauts, 135–36
Australia, mice of, 71–72
Australian National Mouse Club, 85

balance of nature, 73–84
Basil of Baker Street, 33
beavers, 144
BHT, 133–34
biting, 105
black rat *(Rattus rattus), 12,* 12–13, 15, 145
breast cancer, 128, 130
breeding mice, 113–23

brown rat *(Rattus norvegicus),* 13–15, *14,* 145

cages for mice, 94–97, *95, 97*
cancer, 128–30
camouflage, 48–49, 64–65
Carroll, Lewis, 26–27
cat, domestication of, 3
cavies, 144
cheek pouches, 53
chimera mice, 140–41, *141*
China, ancient, 29
chinchillas, 144
chipmunk, 144
Cinderella, 27
classification of rodents, 9–10
*Clethrionomys: see* red-backed mouse
cloning of mouse, 140
collared lemming, 65
commensals, 11, 45–46, 48
common dormouse *(Glis),* 145
community life of house mouse, 38–41
cotton rat *(Sigmodon),* 145
Crete, ancient, 28
Cricetidae, 144

147

cricetids, 9
*Cricetulus* (Chinese hamster): *see* hamster
*Cricetus* (common hamster): *see* hamster
crowding, effects of, 44

deer mouse: *see* white-footed mouse
defenses of house mouse, 43
development of young mice, 116–19, *120, 121*
diabetic mice, 139
diastema, 9
"Dick Whittington and His Cat," 27
*Dicrostonyx: see* snow lemming
diet of mice, 40–41, 103–4, 112
diet research, 132–33
Dipodidae, 145
*Dipodomys: see* kangaroo rat
disease studies, 127–30, 138–39
dormouse *(Glis)*, 26, *26,* 61–62, *62,* 145
drug testing, 127–29, 142

ears of mouse, 17, *17*
ecology, 74–84
Egypt, 3
enemies of house mouse, 42, 45, 46; of other mice, 59, 63–64, 74–76, *75*
environmental impact studies, 80–82
exercise wheel, 97, 98, *99,* 102
eyes of mouse, 16, *17*

fables, mice in, 21–23
fairy tales, mice in, 27

feeding dish, 100
feet of mice, 15
field mouse: *see* meadow vole
fighting among house mice, 38–39, 44
folk tales, mice in, 30–32
food additives, 132–33
"Frog Went A-Courtin, A," 30–32
fur color of mice, 17–18, 47–49, 137

genetics research, 136–41
gerbil, 10, 54–55, *55,* 145
Gerbillinae, 145
*Gerbillus: see* sand rat
germfree research, 130, *131*
Gliridae, 145
*Glis: see* common dormouse
gophers, 144
grasshopper mouse *(Onychomys),* 70, 70–71, 145
gravity, effects on mouse lifetime, 136
Greece, ancient, 4
grooming, 111
guinea pigs, 144

habitat of mice, 50
hairless mouse, 139, *139*
hamster, 10, 144
handedness of mice, 142
handling mice, 105, 107
harvest mouse, 66, *66*
harvest mouse, American *(Reithrodontomys),* 145
harvest mouse, European *(Micromys),* 145

148

hazel mouse *(Muscardinus)*, 145
hearing of mouse, 17
heartbeat of mouse, 104
helpful activities of mice, 79–80
heredity, studies of, 136–41
Heteromyidae, 144
hibernation, 62, 69
house mouse *(Mus musculus)*, 15–19, 145
house mouse, habits of, 38–46
house mouse, origin of, 2–3
house rat, 36–37
human activity, effects on environment, 34, 76–78, 80–84
Hystricomorpha, 9, 144

inbreeding, 125–26

Jackson Laboratory, 138–42
*Jaculus:* see jerboa
jerboa *(Jaculus)*, 69, 69–70, 145
jumping mouse *(Napaeozapus, Zapus)*, 68, 68–69, 145

kangaroo mouse *(Microdipodops)*, 144
kangaroo rat *(Dipodomys)*, 53, 52–54, 144

laboratory mice, 124–43
left-handed mice, 142
lemming, 10, 64–65, 65, 145
*Lemmus:* see Norway lemming
leukemia, 128, 130
life span of mice, 123

litter size, 40, 113–14, 116, 122, 123
live trap, 88
long-tailed tree mouse, 61

marmoset tree mouse, 61
marsupial mice, 71–72, 72
mating, 40
maze, 141
meadow mouse, 44; *see also* meadow vole
meadow vole (meadow mouse) *(Microtus)*, 63–64, 145
memory and learning, 141–43
*Meriones:* see Mongolian gerbil
*Mesocricetus* (golden hamster): *see* hamster
mice, types of, 51
Mickey Mouse, 33, *33*
*Microdipodops:* see kangaroo mouse
*Micromys:* see harvest mouse, European
Microtinae, 145
*Microtus:* see meadow vole
Middle Ages, 29
Mighty Mouse, 33
migration of house mouse, 2, 5–6; of rats, 12–14, of rodents, 14
milk of mouse, *40*, 42
Mongolian gerbil *(Meriones)*, 145
Mother Goose rhymes, 23–26
mouse plagues, 44–45
mousetraps, 3–4
mouse worship, 28
mousy odor, 86–87, 94
Muridae, 145

149

murids, 10
Murinae, 145
*Mus musculus*, 19; see also house mouse
*Muscardinus*: see hazel mouse
muscular dystrophy, 140
muskrat *(Ondatra)*, 145
Myomorpha, 9

*Napaeozapus*: see jumping mice
nature, roles of mice in, 73–84
*Neotoma*: see wood rat
nest box, 98, 99
nest of house mouse, 38–39
New World mice, 10
nocturnal habits, 109
Norway lemming *(Lemmus)*, 145
Norway rat, 14; see also brown rat
nursing of baby mice, *117*, 119

odor trails, 39
odors, mouse reaction to, 16
Old World mice, 10
*Onychomys*: see grasshopper mouse
*Ondatra*: see muskrat
*Oryzomys*: see rice rat

parental care of young, 116–19, 122
*Perognathus*: see pocket mouse
*Peromyscus*: see white-footed mouse
Persia, 4
pests, mice as, 1–5, 73, 77, 85
pets, mice as, 85–123
*Phenacomys*: see tree mouse
Physiognathos, 32

pine mouse *(Pitymys)*, 67, *67*, 145
picking up a mouse, 105–6, *106*
*Pitymys*: see pine mouse
pocket mouse *(Perognathus)*, 48–49, 52–53, *53*, 144
population explosions, 44–45, 76–78
porcupines, 144
prairie dogs, 144
prey, as mice, 74–76
protective coloration, 47–49, 64–65

rats, 10–15, *11*, 78
*Rattus norvegicus*: see brown rat
*Rattus rattus*: see black rat
red-backed mouse *(Clethrionomys)*, *59*, 59–60, 145
red tree mouse, 60–61
*Reithrontomys*: see harvest mouse, American
reproduction of mice, 40, 113–14
reproductive capacity of house mouse, 43–44
Rex mouse, 90, *90*
rice rat *(Oryzomys)*, 145
right-handed mice, 142
rodents, characteristics of, 7–10
Rome, ancient, 4
runaway mice, 87–88

salt march harvest mice, 81, *81*
sand rat *(Gerbillus)*, 145
scent marking, 39, 87
Sciuromorpha, 9, 144
scotophobin, 143

*Sigmodon:* see cotton rat
skin transplants, 126
sleeping, 109, 111
smell, sense of, 39–40
snow lemming *(Dicrostonyx),* 64–65, 145
space research, 135–36
spiny mouse *(Acomys),* 55–57, 145
squeaks of mouse, 17
squirrels, 144
Strabo, 4
Stuart Little, 32–33
superstitions, 27–29
survival of animals and plants, 34–37
survival of rodents, 47–50
sexing a mouse, *93,* 93–94
sex ratio in litters, 123

tail of mouse, *15,* 15–16
teeth of rodent, *8,* 8–9
territorial behavior of mouse, 38–40
tetanus, 105
thymus gland, 134–35
Tom and Jerry, 33
tooth decay, 130, 138
toys for mice, 101–2, 109, *110*
tree mouse *(Phenacomys),* 145
tricks, teaching, 107–8

urine of mice, 86–87

varieties of laboratory mice, 124–26, *125,* 138–39
varieties of mice, 88–90
vesper mouse: *see* white-footed mouse
viruses and cancer, 129–30
vitamin A, 129
vitamin E, 134

waltzing mouse, 90
"War of Frogs and Mice, The," 32
washing, 111
water, conservation of, 41–42, 54, 55
water supply, 100–101
whiskers of mouse, 17, *17*
white-footed mouse *(Peromyscus),* 57–59, *58,* 145
White Sands National Monument, 48–49
witchcraft, mice and, 29
*Wizard of Oz,* the, 23
woodchucks, 144
wood mouse: *see* white-footed mouse
wood rat *(Neotoma),* 144

X rays, 129

yellow-necked mouse *(Apodemus),* 60, 145

Zapodidae, 145
*Zapus: see* jumping mouse

ALVIN SILVERSTEIN grew up in Brooklyn, New York, and developed an early interest in science. He received his B.A. from Brooklyn College, his M.S. from the University of Pennsylvania, and his Ph.D. from New York University. He is Professor of Biology at the College of Staten Island of the City University of New York.

VIRGINIA B. SILVERSTEIN, a native of Philadelphia, received her B.A. from the University of Pennsylvania. Since her marriage, she has worked as a free-lance translator of Russian scientific literature, doing extensive work for government and private agencies.

The Silversteins, who have collaborated on over fifty science books for young readers, live on a farm in Hunterdon County, New Jersey, with their six children.

ROBERT A. SILVERSTEIN, born in Brooklyn, New York, and transplanted to rural New Jersey, is majoring in Human Communications at Rutgers University. He plans a career emphasizing his interests in nature, writing, and photography.